ARE YOU READY FOR WAR?

by

J.V. Simpson-Linder

ISBN: 978-1-59352-337-4

Published by:
Christian Services Network
833 Broadway, Suite #201
El Cajon, CA 92021
Toll Free: 1-866-484-6184
www.CSNbooks.com

Unless otherwise stated all Scripture is taken from the King James Version of the Bible.

Printed in the United States of America.

TABLE OF CONTENTS

DEDICATION

This book is dedicated to the memory of my father, Rev. A. B. Simpson, who 'fought the good fight and finished the race' (1915 - 2006) and my mother, Helen Simpson, who taught me that I could do anything that I was called to do (1919-2007). Thank you, Mom and Dad.

Acknowledgements

A special "thank you" to Ms. Marilyn Todd-Daniels who so graciously allowed me to use her painting "Victory" for the cover on this book.

I also wish to thank all the family and friends for their encouragement during the process of this endeavor.

INTRODUCTION

There are three intertwined truths revealed in the Book of Ephesians. Each truth builds upon the previous truth.

The first three chapters of Ephesians teach the believer's exalted position in Jesus Christ.

The <u>first</u> teaching reveals what Christ has done for the believer. Everyone who has received Christ as Savior has an exalted position.

The <u>second</u> teaching, as emphasized in the last three chapters of Ephesians, concerns the believer's spiritual walk on this earth based on his position in Christ, by addressing what Christ wants to accomplish in the believer's life.

<u>Lastly,</u> Ephesians concludes by teaching about the believer's spiritual conflict. This gives us a picture of how Christ is seen working through the believer.

You might ask, "Why end the epistle in conflict?"

It does seem strange that after the book sets forth the exalted position each believer has in Christ and the victorious walk that every believer is supposed to obtain, it then ends in warfare.

It is stated that Christ has already won the victory for the believer.

> *...when he ascended on high, he led captivity captive, and gave gifts to men*
>
> (Ephesians 4:8)

Simply stated, it means that He led those captives who died prior to His coming, out of their state of captivity (spiritual death). So, if we are victorious in Him, why the conflict?

It is our nature to want to always be on the "mountaintop". Peter, James and John experienced this same desire when they witnessed the transfiguration of the Lord and Him talking with Elijah and Moses. It was such a thrilling experience that Peter said to the Lord,

> ...*it is good for us to be here. If thou wilt, let us make here three tabernacles; one for thee, and one for Moses, and one for Elias'.*
>
> (Matthew 17:4)

But it could not be done. They had to return to the valley. All of us must return to the valley and our duties of life and to serve Christ in these activities. It is true we need the mountaintop experiences...but we cannot live there.

CHAPTER ONE

Reasons for Spiritual Conflict

There are three reasons why a believer can expect – and must be prepared for – a spiritual conflict as he lives for the Lord.

<u>First:</u> Believers must be prepared for spiritual warfare because there is a traitor in the camp. This traitor is the "Flesh", which is the old nature. The old nature is not eradicated when a person receives Christ as Savior, so there is a spiritual struggle between the old nature and the new nature in the life of each believer.

For the flesh lusteth against the Spirit, and the Spirit against the flesh: and these are contrary one to the other.

(Galatians 5:17)

Here we see the flesh opposing the liberty we have in Christ. The flesh always seeks to bring us into bondage to its' desires. Satan entices us through the flesh. Jesus had to rebuke Peter one time by saying,

> *Simon, Simon, behold Satan hath desired to have you, that he may sift you as wheat: but I have prayed for thee, that thy faith fail not.*
> (Luke 22:31, 32)

Satan is the enemy of our soul; he is envious of our salvation in Christ and especially seeks to destroy our allegiance to Christ. Satan trails believers and tries to take advantage of them. The Bible tells us,

> *Be sober, be vigilant: because your adversary the devil, as a roaring lion, walketh about, seeking whom he may devour. Whom resist steadfast in the faith, knowing that the same afflictions are accomplished in your brethren that are in the world.*
> (1 Peter 5:8, 9)

<u>Second:</u> The reason for spiritual conflict is that the believer is a member of the body of Christ. From the time that God cursed Satan in the Garden of Eden, Satan has tried to destroy Christ. Therefore, anyone associated with Christ – especially a part of His body – is subject to Satan's attack. There are many recorded instances throughout the scriptures when Satan tried to destroy Christ. When Christ chose to become born of man and to die for man's sin, Satan determined to destroy Him. While Christ was a baby, Herod served Satan's purpose when he gave the decree that all children in Bethlehem and surrounding areas, two years old and under, should be killed.

> *Then Herod, when he saw that he was mocked of the wise men, was exceeding wroth, and sent forth , and*

slew all the children that were in Bethlehem, and in all the coasts thereof, from two years old and under...

(Matthew 2:16)

Jesus escaped death because Mary and Joseph had been instructed by God to take Him out of the country.

... the angel of the Lord appeareth to Joseph in a dream, saying, 'arise, take the young child and his mother and flee into Egypt.

(Matthew 2:13)

Later, when Satan tried to entice Jesus to sin, by challenging him to throw himself down from a pinnacle of the temple, Christ responded,

Jesus said unto him, 'It is written again, thou shalt not tempt the Lord your God.

(Matthew 4:7)

When Jesus was on the cross, Satan no doubt thought he was victorious in having Christ put to death. When Christ rose from the dead, he thereby proved that he had conquered Satan. Christ then ascended to the Father, beyond the reach of Satan.

As Satan can no longer attack Christ, he attacks the body of Christ which is the church of believers. The mystical body of Christ, made-up of believers, is within the reach of Satan even though Christ himself is not. However, the body of Christ will ultimately be victorious, for Christ said,

And I say also unto thee, that thou art Peter, and upon this rock I will build my church; and the gates of hell shall not prevail against it.

(Matthew 16:18)

13

<u>Third</u>: The reason there is spiritual conflict for believers is that God's plan and purpose include the fact that Christ will someday rule the world in righteousness. Because this refers to a future time, this might be referred to as a "dispensational" reason for spiritual conflict. As the apostle John told of a vision he had of Christ's return to earth, he said,

...and I saw heaven opened and behold a white horse; and he that sat upon him was called Faithful and True.

(Revelation 19:11)

Because he hath appointed a day, in the which he will judge the world in righteousness by that man whom he hath ordained; whereof he hath given assurance unto all men, in that he hath raised him from the dead.

(Acts 17:31)

This verse reveals that the Father has delegated all judgment to the Son. This means – and Satan knows this – that there will be a final reckoning with the powers of evil, which will result in their – and Satan's – ultimate destruction.

In (Revelation 1:18) Christ says,

I am he that liveth, and was dead, and behold, I am alive forevermore, Amen; and have the keys of hell and of death.

The final doom of Satan is told in:

And the devil that deceived them, was cast into the lake of fire and brimstone, where the beast and false prophet are, and shall be tormented day and night for ever and ever.

(Revelation 20:10)

Inasmuch as believers are to share with Christ in his reigning and judging, we are laid open to the attacks of Satan at the present time. Satan and his messenger claim this world as their own; thus, those of us who will eventually sit in judgment over them are placed in a position of conflict. Satan is well aware that God's program is closing in on him and for this reason he directs much of his attention to harassing the church. Even though Satan is at work, the Holy Spirit is at present restraining evil.

For the mystery of iniquity doth already work; only he who not letteth will let, until he be taken out of the way.

(2 Thessalonians 2:7)

This restraining work of the Holy Spirit, through believers, has been going on ever since the day of Pentecost when the church came into existence. But it is evident we are being brought ever nearer to the final conflict. Therefore, as Paul wrote in his letter to the Ephesians, the final remarks concerning the believer's warfare were necessary and right on target. Believers ought not to be controlled by fear because of this warfare. Rather, we should remember the words of,

...I will build my church; and the gates of hell shall not prevail against it.

(Matthew 16:18)

...In the world ye shall have tribulation: but be of good cheer; I have overcome the world.

(John 16:33)

...Greater is He that is in you, than he that is the world.

(1 John 4:4)

15

The Christian does not need to live in constant fear of Satan and his minions.

If God be for us, who can be against us.

(Romans 8:31)

Paul was writing to believers and the word "IF" has the meaning of "SINCE". That is, those of us who have received Jesus Christ as Savior know that God is for us because Paul has told us this in the preceding passages. Therefore, since God is for us no one is able to stand against us. Paul further explained, in:

He who did not spare his own Son, but gave him up for us all – how will he not also, along with him, graciously give us all things?

(Romans 8:32)

This is where we stand! This is our position in Christ. Thus Paul said in:

"Who shall lay anything to the charge of God's elect? It is God that justifieth. Who is he that condemns? Christ Jesus, who died – more than that, who was raised to life – is at the right hand of God and is also interceding for us.

(Romans 8:33-34)

The devil cannot effectively charge us with something now because, having believed in Jesus Christ as Savior, we have been justified – declared righteous. Though the devil may bring accusation, Jesus Christ is at the right hand of the Father interceding for us. The Lord Jesus Christ has paid the full penalty for our sin, so the devil – or anyone else – is not able to bring condemnation on us.

With these three truths in mind concerning our position in Christ, let us focus on

16

Ephesians 6:10-20:

This passage refers to the spiritual warfare in which every believer is involved. It reveals the source of the strength and the weapons we have that enable us to be victorious. We must understand clearly the principles by which this warfare is to be fought. There are certain conditions that must be met if we are to personally experience the victory that Christ has already accomplished for us. It is important to recognize that victory is "assumed". Christ has defeated Satan and has won the victory for us. Therefore, our responsibility is to live according to our victorious position and not to suffer defeat at the hands of the enemy, who has already been defeated! We are to take our stand against any trial or attack Satan will throw at us because he has no chance to defeat us as long as we recognize our position in Christ.

Victory for the believer is the valid promise on which everything else is based. This is seen as Paul asked the question,

> *Who shall separate us from the love of Christ?*
> (Romans 8:35)

After mentioning some things that could be considered possibilities, Paul gave this resounding answer:

> *No, in all these things we are more than conquerors through him who loved us.*
> (Romans 8:37)

> *...nor anything else in all creation will be able to separate us from the love of God that is in Christ Jesus our Lord.*
> (Romans 8:39)

17

How can we be more than conquerors? This will be revealed as we examine Ephesians 6:10-20. How wonderful it is to know that nothing can separate us from the love of God. Through these verses Paul reveals God's all-sufficient provision for such total victory. Paul also reminded the Corinthians of the victory we have in Christ in:

But thanks be to God, which giveth us the victory through our Lord Jesus Christ.

(1 Corinthians 15:57)

But thanks be unto God, which always causeth us to triumph in Christ.

(1 Corinthians 2:14)

Ephesians 6:10-20 reveals God's all-sufficient provision for such total victory.

CHAPTER TWO

The Believer's Strength for the Conflict

Finally, my brethren, be strong in the Lord, and in the power of His might.

(Ephesians 6:10)

The Christian's life is frequently represented in the scriptures under the metaphor of warfare. Christ is called "The Captain of His Salvation"; and they who have enlisted under His banners and 'Quit themselves like me', fighting the good fight of faith', and enduring cheerfully all the hardships of the campaign, are called 'good soldiers of Jesus Christ'. Like warriors, they do not entangle themselves with the affairs of this life that they may please Him who has chosen them to be soldiers; but they set themselves to 'war a good warfare', and they look for the rewards of victory when they have subdued all their enemies. In the chapter before us, this subject is not slightly touched, as the attached passages above referred to, but is treated at large; and that which in other places is only a metaphor is here a professed simile. Paul, standing as it were in the midst of the camp, harangues the soldiers, telling them what enemies they have to combat, and how they may guard effectually against all their stratagems, and secure to themselves the victory.

He begins with an animating exhortation, in which he reminds them to place the most unlimited confidence in his skill and power. The exhortation being contracted into a very small space, and conveying far more than appears at first sight, we shall consider, first; "What is implied in it".

WHAT IS IMPLIED IN THE EXHORTATION?

1. The Christian has need of strength

The first thing that would naturally occur to anyone to whom this exhortations was addressed is that the Christian has need of strength; for, on any other supposition than this, the words would be altogether absurd; but, the Christian will indeed appear to require strength, whether we consider the work he has to perform, or the difficulties he has to cope with. It is no easy matter to stem the tide of corrupt nature, to control the impetuous passions, to root out inveterate habits, to turn the current of our affections from the things of time and sense to things invisible and eternal. To renew and sanctify our heart, and to transform them into the divine image, in a work far beyond the power of feeble man; yet it is indispensably necessary to his salvation.

As though this were not of itself sufficient to call forth the Christian's exertions, he has hosts of enemies to contend with, as soon as ever he addresses himself in earnest

20

to the work assigned him. Not to mention all the propensities of his nature, which will instantly rise up in rebellion against him, and exert all their power for the master, the world will immediately begin to cry out against him; they will direct all their artillery against him, their scoffs, their ridicule, their threats; his very friends will turn against him and; 'those of his own household will become his greatest foes'. They would let him go on in the broad road year after year, and not one amongst them would ever exhort him to love and serve his God; but the very moment that he enters on the narrow path that leads to life, they will all, with one heart and one soul, unite their endeavors to obstruct his course; and, when they cannot prevail, they will turn their back upon him, and give him up as an irreclaimable enthusiast.

In conjunction with these will Satan (as we shall hereafter have occasion to show) combine his forces; yes, he will put himself at their head, and direct their motions, and stimulate their exertions, and concur with them to the uttermost to captivate and destroy the heaven-born soul.

Can such work be performed, such difficulties be surmounted, without the greatest efforts? Surely they who are called to such things had need 'to be strong'.

2. The Christian has no strength in himself

If the Christian had strength in himself, why should he be exhorted to be strong in another?

Little do men imagine how extremely impotent they are in themselves to do that which is good. It must be easy, one would suppose, to read and understand the word of God, or, at least, to profit by a clear and faithful ministration of it.

But these are far beyond the power of the natural man. The word is a 'sealed book' to him, which, for want of a spiritual discernment, appears a mass of foolishness, a 'cunningly devised fable.' Even when it was explained by our Lord, the apostles, for the space of more than three years, were not able to comprehend its' import, till He opened their understandings to understand it; and Lydia, like thousands of others, would have been unmoved by the preaching of Paul, if the Lord had not 'opened her heart' to apprehend and embrace His word. It should seem, however, that if these things are beyond the power of man, he can at least pray to God to instruct him. But neither can he do this, unless the spirit of God 'help his infirmities,' teaching him what to pray for, and assisting him in offering the petitions.

If he is insufficient for this work, it may be hoped he is able to do something. However, our Lord tells us that, without the special aid of his grace, he 'can do nothing'. Can he not then speak what is good? No.

...how can you who are evil say anything good?'
(Matthew 12:34)

And Paul says,

...and no one can say, "Jesus is Lord," except by the Holy Spirit.'
(1 Corinthians 12:3)

Still, may he not will, or at least think, what is good? We must answer this also in the negative.

It is God (alone) who worketh in you both to will and to do of His good pleasure.
(2 Corinthians 3:5)

Nor had Paul himself, no, not even after his conversions, an ability of himself, to think anything good: his sufficiency was of God and of God alone. Our impotence cannot be more fitly expressed by any words whatever than by that expression of the apostle;

Ye are dead in trespasses and sins.

(Ephesians 2:1-2)

Until God quickens us from the dead, we are as incapable of all the exercises of the spiritual life as a breathless corpse is of all the functions of the animal life.

3. There is sufficiency for us in Christ

There is sufficiency in Christ; for otherwise Paul would not have urged us in this manner to be strong in Him.

Well does the apostle speak of Christ's mighty power for indeed he is Almighty,

He has all power committed to Him both in heaven and earth.

(Matthew 28:18)

We may judge of his all-sufficiency by what he wrought when he was on earth: The most inveterate diseases vanished at his touch. At his word, a mere act of volition, when he was at a distance from the patient. The fishes of the sea were constrained to minister unto him. Even the devils themselves yielded to His authority, and were instantly forced to liberate their captives at His command. They could not even enter into the swine without his permission. The very elements also were obedient to His word. The winds were stilled. The waves ceased to roll. The storm that threatened to overwhelm Him became a perfect calm.

23

What then can He not do for those who trust in Him? Is His hand now shortened, that He cannot save? Or is His ear deaf that He cannot hear?

> *Can He not heal the diseases of our souls, and calm our troubled spirits, and supply our every want?*
>
> (Isaiah 59:1)

> *Cannot He who triumphed over principalities and powers upon the cross, and spoiled them, and let them captive in His ascension, fulfill His promise, that sin shall not have dominion over us, and that Satan shall be bruised under our feet shortly.*
>
> (Colossians 2:15; Psalms 68:18; Ephesians 4:8)

> *Doubtless He is The Lord Jehovah, in whom is everlasting strength, and who is therefore able to save the uttermost all that come unto God by Him.*
>
> (Isaiah 2:4; Hebrews 7:25)

These things being understood as implied in the exhortation, we may more fully comprehend, in the second place, what is expressed in it.

It is evident that there are two points to which the apostle designs to lead us: The one is to rely on Christ for strength, the other is to 'Be strong in Him,' and with assured confidence of success.

In relation to the first of these we observe that a general must confide in his army quite as much as his army confides in him. They cannot move to advantage without an experienced head to guide them, so neither can he succeed in his plans, unless he have a brave and well appointed

24

army to carry them into execution. It is not this way in the Christian army. There all the confidence is in the General alone. He must not only train his soldiers and direct them in the day of battle, but he must be with them in the battle, shielding their heads, strengthening their arms, animating their courage, reviving them when faint, raising them when fallen, healing them when wounded, and finally, beating down their enemies that they may trample them under feet.

The fullness that is in Christ is treasured up in Him for us that we may receive out of it according to our necessities. As He came down from heaven to purchase for us all the gifts of the spirit, so He has ascended up to heaven that He might bestow them upon us, and fill us, each according to His measure, with all the fullness of God. Hence, previous to His death He said,

> *Ye believe in God; believe also in me.*
>
> (John 14:1)

Let that same faith you repose in God the Father, as your creator, be reposed in me as your redeemer. Let it be full, and implicit. Let it extend to every want. Let it be firm and unshaken under all circumstances, however difficult, however adverse.

Such was our Lord's direction. Agreeable to it was the experience of the great apostle, who says,

> *The life which I now live by the faith of the Son of God, who loved me, and gave himself for me.*
>
> (Galatians 2:20)

It is characteristic of every Christian solder to receive thus out of Christ's fullness, and to say,

In the Lord have I righteousness and strength.
(Isaiah 45:24)

The principal point which the apostle aims at in the text is to inspire us with a holy confidence in Christ, so that we may be as much assured of victory as if we saw all our enemies fleeing before us, or already prostrate at our feet. We cannot have a more striking illustration of our duty in this respect than the history of David's combat with Goliath. He would not go against his adversary with armor suited to the occasion. He went forth in the name of the God of Israel, and therefore he did not doubt one moment the issue of the contest. He well knew that God could direct his aim, and that he was as sure of victory without any other arms than a sling and a stone from his shepherd's bag as he could be with the most complete armor that Saul, himself, could give him.

What David thus illustrated, we may see exemplified in the conduct of Paul;

If God be for us, who can be against us? I fear none of them, since Christ has died, yea rather risen again, and maketh intercession for me. Who shall separate us from the love of Christ? Shall tribulation, or distress, or persecution, or famine, or nakedness, or peril, or sword? Nay, in all these things we are more than conquerors through Him that loved us. For I am persuaded that neither death, nor life, nor angels, nor principalities, nor powers, not things present, nor things to come, nor height, nor depth, nor any other creature, shall be able to separate us from the love of God, which is in Christ Jesus our Lord.

(Romans 8:31-39)

26

Thus it is that we must go forth against all the enemies of our salvation. We must, 'have no confidence in the flesh'; neither must we have any doubt in our God. The weakest amongst us should boldly say,

The Lord is my helper; I will not fear what men or devils can do against me; I can do all things through Christ who strengtheneth me.
                              (Hebrews 13:6; Philippians 4:13)

In applying this subject to the different classes of professing Christians, we shall first address ourselves to the self-confident.

It is the solemn declaration of God, that:

By strength shall no man prevail.

                              (1 Samuel 2:9)

We might hope that men would be convinced of this truth by their own experience. Who amongst us has not made vows and resolutions without number, and broken them again almost as soon as they were made? Who ever resolved to devote himself unfeigned to God, and did not find that he was unable steadfastly to pursue his purpose? What folly is it then to be renewing these vain attempts, when we have the evidence both of scripture and experience that we cannot succeed! How much better would it be to trust in that mighty one, on whom help is laid!

Learn, brethren, before it be too late, that without Christ you can do nothing, that all your fresh springs are in Him, and of Him must your fruit be found: In Him alone shall all the seed of Israel be justified, and shall glory. If you will not be strong in Him, you will continue without

27

strength; but, if once you truly know Him, you shall be strong and do exploits.

(John 15:5)

We would next claim the attention of the timid. It is but too common for the Lord's people to be indulging needless fears, like David when he said,

I shall one day perish by the hand of Saul.

(1 Samuel 17:1)

But surely such deserve the rebuke which our Lord gave to Peter.

O, thou of little faith, wherefore didst thou doubt?

(Matthew 14:3)

If you doubt the Lord's willingness to save you, did he not die for the most chief of sinners? If you call into question His power, what is there in your case that can baffle omnipotence? If you are discouraged on account of your own weakness, do you not know the weaker you are in yourself, the stronger you shall be in Him, and that He will perfect His own strength in your weakness? If you fear on account of the strength and number of your enemies, He meets your fear with this salutary admonition.

Do not call conspiracy everything that these people call conspiracy; do not fear what they fear, and do not dread it. The Lord Almighty is the one you are to regard as holy, he is the one you are to fear, he is the one you are to dread...

(Isaiah 8:12-13)

Only trust in Him; and though weak, He will strengthen you; though faint, He will revive you; though wounded, he will heal you; though captive, He will liberate you;

though slain, He will raise you up again, and give you victory over all your enemies. Be strong then and very courageous; abhor the thought of indulging a cowardly spirit as long as "God's throne is in heaven"; and assure yourselves with David,

> *They surround me on every side, but in the name of the Lord I cut them off. They swarmed me like bees, but they died out as quickly as burning thorns; ...*

(Psalm 118: 11-12)

4. Let the victorious Christian listen to a word of counsel.

We are apt to be elated in the time of victory, and to arrogate to ourselves some portion of the glory. But God solemnly cautions us against this: And if, with Nebuchadnezzar and Sennacherib, we take glory to ourselves, the time is nigh at hand when God will fearfully abase us. We cannot do better than take the psalmist for our pattern. He was enabled to perform the most astonishing feats, and was honored with the most signal victories; yet so careful is he to give the glory to God that he repeats again and again the same grateful acknowledgment, confessing God to be the sole author of his success, and ascribing to him the honor due unto his name. Let it be remembered, that our enemies still live and are mighty; and therefore we must not boast as if the time were come for us to put off our armor. We need the same power to keep down our enemies, as bringing them down at first. We should soon fall a prey to the tempter, if left one moment to ourselves. Let our eyes therefore still be to Jesus, 'the author and finisher of our faith,' depending on His mighty power for 'strength according to our day,' and for the accomplishment of the promise which He hath give us, that

>   *...no weapon formed against us shall prosper.*
>   (Hebrews 12:2; Deuteronomy 33:25; Isaiah 54:17)

CHAPTER THREE

The Means of Withstanding Satan's Wiles

*Put on the full armor of God, so that you can take
your stand against the devil's schemes.*

(Ephesians 6:11)

The devil himself is the primary foe of the believer.
From the passage above we see that even the world system
and the flesh are enemies of the believer. The key figure in
the spiritual conflict that the believer must face is Satan.
So the conflict of Ephesians 6 does not come from within...
but from without the believer. Paul gave instructions ear-
lier in Ephesians as to how the internal enemy of the flesh
was to be dealt with. These instructions were given specifically in:

*You were taught in regard to your former way of
life, to put off your old self, which is being cor-
rupted by its' deceitful desires, to be made new in
the attitude of your minds.*

(Ephesians 4:22-24)

31

If we have done what Paul said to do, we can treat self, or the flesh, as a conquered foe. However, we must remember that the desires of the old nature continually seek out attention, so we must always be on our guard concerning the flesh.

Having been faithful in overcoming the internal foe, we can now turn our attention toward overcoming the external foe. If, however, we have come to grips with the problem of self, we are in position to maintain victory over Satan. The old testament Israelites serve as a national parallel to this individual problem. After the Israelites were delivered from Egypt, they wandered in the desert, being preoccupied with themselves and murmuring against God. During the years of wandering they were ineffective for God because they refused to take him at his word and go into Canaan and conquer the land. The older generation died in the wilderness because of their disobedience, but the new generation believed God, left the desert behind them and entered the land God had promised them. There they engaged in warfare against God's and their common enemies, for even though God had promised them the land they had to act on faith and take it. They were able to effectively stand against their enemies only as they overcame preoccupation with themselves.

So, too, Satan has no need to attack us as long as we are preoccupied with self.

However, when we take God at his word and walk in faith, we can be sure that we will be exposed to, and experience, the attacks of Satan. Of course, the believer can avoid much spiritual conflict by remaining in a spiritual desert even as Israel remained in the desert rather than believing God and engaging in warfare. But if the believer fails to move out for the Lord, he will never know the joy of spiritual victory the Lord desires him to know. There may be conflict but it will be the conflict of the believer's will with God's will, not the spiritual conflict that is referred to in Ephesians 6.

The warfare described in Ephesians 6:10-20 is a warfare in which we join the Lord in holding the position of victory that he has already secured. We need not yield to fear concerning Satan for Christ has been victorious over him and our need is to claim our position of victory in Christ.

Those of us who trust in Him as Savior become part of his mystical body, the church. Those who have not yet believed are in a sense bound by Satan because they have been blinded by him.

> *And even if our gospel is veiled, it is veiled to those who are perishing. The god of this age has blinded the minds of the unbelievers, so that they cannot see the light of the gospel of the glory of Christ...*
>
> (2 Corinthians 4:3-4)

Our responsibility as believers is to pray for these who are blinded by Satan, for in this way we engage in spiritual warfare and stand with Christ in overcoming Satan; that is, in binding the strong man.

> *...how can anyone enter a strong man's house and carry off his possessions unless he first ties up the strong man?*
>
> (Matthew 12:29)

Notice that there is no neutral position – people are either for Christ or against him. It is impossible to maintain a middle of the road position concerning one's relationship with Jesus Christ.

He who is not with me is against me, and he who does not gather with me scatters.

(Matthew 12:30)

To be possessed of courage is not the only requisite for a good soldier; he must be skilled in the use of arms; he must be acquainted with those stratagems which his adversaries will use for his destruction; he must know how to repel an assault, and how in his turn to assault his enemy; in short, he must be trained to war. Nor will his knowledge avail him any thing, unless he stand armed for the combat. Hence the apostle, having encouraged the Christian soldier, and inspired him with confidence in 'The Captain of his salvation,' now calls him to put on his armor, and, by skilful use of it, to prepare for the day of battle.

The real enemy is not visible; he is a mighty but unseen foe. However, he expresses himself through that which is visible; whether it is people or circumstances. We are warring not only against Satan, but also against his hosts,

For we wrestle not against flesh and blood, but against principalities, against powers, against the rulers of the darkness of this world, against spiritual wickedness in high places.

(Ephesians 6:12, KJV)

Let us look at the Hebrew/Greek translation of this passage.

34

1. Wrestle: 'eimi – pale' "I exist / to vibrate" (against)

2) Principalities: 'arche' "chief (in various applications of order, time, place, or rank) KJV- at the beginning, corner, magistrate, power.

3) Powers: 'exousia' "in the sense of ability; (subjectively) force, capacity, competency (objectively) mastery, superhuman, potentate, delegated influence. KJV – authority, jurisdiction, right

4) Rulers: 'kosmokrator' "a world ruler, an epithet of Satan KJV – ruler

5) Darkness: 'skotos' "to obscure or blind" KJV – be full of darkness

6) Spiritual: 'pneumatikos' "non-carnal, (humanly) ethereal. (demoniacally) a spirit (divinely) supernatural, regenerate, religious KJV – spiritual

7) Wickedness: 'poneria' "depravity, malice, plots, sins" KJV – iniquity

8) High: 'epuranios' "above the sky" KJV – celestial, heaven

9) Take unto You: 'analambano' "to take up" KJV- receive up

Man-made weapons are of no advantage in this spiritual warfare.

2 Corinthians 10:3-5 reminds us *"For though we live in the world, we do not wage war as the world does."* The weapons we fight with are not the weapons of the world. On the contrary they have divine power to demolish strong-

holds. We demolish arguments and every pretension that sets itself up against the knowledge of God, and we take captive every thought to make it obedient to Christ."

The hosts of Satan are fallen angels who do his bidding. Although Satan is not omnipresent, his will is carried out on a universal scale through his emissaries. He is their commander in chief. These hosts of fallen angels are referred to as principalities and powers in Ephesians 6:12. This indicates that the messengers of Satan are a well-organized army divided into ranks and divisions. "Principalities" is literally "Rulers", and "Powers" is literally "Authorities". Thus, principalities and powers refer to the supremacy of rule and authority in the satanic realm. The words 'rulers of the darkness' of this world are literally the world rulers of this darkness. No wonder it is said that our *"warfare is against spiritual wickedness in high places"* (vs. 12)

The Greek word translated "high places" in Ephesians 6:12 is the same word that is translated "Heavenly Places" in Ephesians 1:3, 20; 2:6, and 3:10. Although the heavenly realm is referred to in both instances, a different sphere of heaven is intended.:

> *I know a man in Christ who fourteen years ago was caught up to the third heaven.*
> (2 Corinthians 12:2)

We learn from Paul, in the above scripture, that there are three heavens, for Paul referred to a person – probably himself – who was "caught up to the third heaven". The third heaven is the place of God's special abode, the second in the stellar heaven, and the first is the atmospheric heaven, which is closest to earth.

36

Although principalities and powers are in a heavenly realm, the believer's position with Christ is higher than these, for Ephesians 1:20-21 tells us that the father set Christ,

> *...at his own right hand in the heavenly places, far above all principality, and power, and might, and dominion, and every name that is named, not only in this world, but also in that which is to come.*

It is the third (3rd) heaven that Christ referred to as, *"my father's house"* (John 14:2) and it is there that we have our spiritual position with Christ; therefore, in him we too are situated above these satanic forces in spiritual authority. This is our position by faith.

There was a time when Satan – then known as Lucifer – lived in the third heaven with God.

> *How you have fallen from heaven, O morning star, son of the dawn! You have been cast down to the earth, you who once laid low the nations!*
> (Isaiah 14:12-14)

Satan does not dwell in the third heaven although he has access to it to accuse those who have faith in God:

> *One day the angels came to present themselves before the Lord, and Satan also came with them. The Lord said to Satan, 'where have you come from?' Satan answered the Lord, 'From roaming through the earth and going back and forth in it.' On another day the angels came to present themselves before the Lord, and Satan also came with them to present himself before him.*
> (Job 1:6-12; 2:1-7)

37

Having been thrown out of the third heaven, the place of God's abode, Satan now has domain in the first and second heavens – the atmospheric and stellar heavens. He is known as the *'Prince of the power of the air'* (Ephesians 2:2).

Even a casual acquaintance with scripture reveals that Satan is much more than an influence; he is a person, and as such, he speaks, he plans, he deceives, he hates, he fights. Yet some people refuse to believe that the devil is a real person, maintaining that he is only the influence of evil, or a symbol of evil. Even this misconception is a tribute to Satan's success in deceiving unbelievers. One of his best methods of concealing his activities is to influence people to think that he does not exist. A false optimism appears wherever Satan is not recognized as the key enemy working in human affairs.

To open fully the direction before us, we must show you, first, "the wiles of the devil," and next, "the means of defeating them."

We shall endeavor to lay before you "the wiles of the devil".

Satan is the great adversary of God and man, and labors to the uttermost to destroy the interests of both. In prosecuting his purpose, he has two grand objects in view; <u>to lead men into sin and to keep them from God.</u> We must consider these distinctly and point out the stratagems he uses for the attainment of his ends.

To Lead Men Into Sin

To effect this, he presents to them such temptations as are best suited to their natural dispositions. A skillful general will not attempt to storm a fort on the side that is impregnable. Rather, he will direct his efforts against the weaker parts, where he has a better prospect of success. Therefore, Satan considers the weak part of each and every man and directs his artillery where he may most easily make a breach. He well knew the covetous dispositions of Judas and of Ananias and Sapphira when he wanted the one to betray his master and the others to bring discredit on the Christian name. He wrought upon their natural propensities, and instigated them with ease to the execution of his will. Thus, he stimulates the proud or passionate, the lewd or covetous, the timid or melancholy, to such acts as are most congenial with their feelings, to the intent that his agency may be least discovered and his purposes most effectually secured.

Much craft is also discoverable in the seasons in which he chooses for making his assaults. If a general knew that his adversaries were harassed with fatigue, or reveling and intoxicated amidst the spoils of victory, or separated from the main body of their army so that they could have no support, he would not fail to take advantage of such circumstances, rather than attack them when they were in full force and in a state of readiness for the combat.

Such a general is Satan. If he finds us in a state of great trouble and perplexity, when the spirits are exhausted, the mind clouded, the strength enervated, then he will seek to draw us to murmuring or despair. Thus he acted towards

Christ himself when he had been fasting forty days and forty nights, and again on the eve of his crucifixion. The former of these occasions afforded him a favorable opportunity for tempting our blessed Lord to despondency, to presumption, to a total alienation of his heart from God. The latter inspired him with a hope of drawing our Lord to some act unworthy of his high character and subversive of the ends for which he came into the world.

Again, if we have been elevated with peculiar joy, he well knows how apt we are to relax our vigilance, and to indulge a carnal security. Hence, immediately on Paul's descent from the third heavens, the paradise of God, Satan strove to puff him up with pride that he might bring him into the condemnation of the devil. With even more success did he assault Peter immediately after the most exalted honor had been conferred upon him, whereby he brought upon the unguarded saint that just rebuke.

> *Get behind me, Satan! You are a stumbling block to me, you do not have in mind the things of God, but the things of men.*
> (Matthew 16:23)

Above all, Satan is sure to embrace an opportunity when we are alone, withdrawn from those whose eye would intimidate or whose counsel would restrain us. He could not prevail on Lot, when in the midst of Sodom, to violate the rights of hospitality; but, when he was in a retired cave, he too successfully tempted him to repeated acts of drunkenness and incest. And who amongst us has not found that seasons of privacy, or at least, of seclusion from those who know us, have been times of more than ordinary temptation?

The means which Satan uses in order to accomplish his purpose will afford us a yet further insight into his wiles. Whom will a general so soon employ to betray the enemy into his hands, as one who by his power can command them, or by his professions can deceive them? And is it not thus with Satan? If he wants to draw down the judgments of God upon the whole nation of the Jews, he will stir up David, in spite of all the expostulations of his courtiers, to number the people. If he would destroy Ahab, he becomes a lying spirit in the mouth of Ahab's prophets to persuade him, and by him to lead Jehoshaphat also and the combined armies into the most imminent peril. Would he have Job to curse his God? No fitter person to employ on this service than Job's own wife, whom he taught to give this counsel. *"Curse God, and die!"* (Job 2:9)

Would he prevail on Jesus to lay aside the thoughts of suffering for the sins of men? His friend, Peter, must offer him this advice. *"Master, spare thyself"* (Matthew 16:22).

Thus in leading us to the commission of sin, he will use sometimes the authority of magistrates, of masters, or of parents, and sometimes the influence of our dearest friends or relatives. No instrument is so fit for him as those of man's own household.

There is also something further observable in the manner in which Satan tempts the soul. An able general will study to conceal the main object of his attack, and by feints to deceive his enemy. Thus does Satan form his attack with all imaginable cunning. His mode of beguiling Eve will serve as a specimen of his artifices in every age. He first only enquired whether any prohibition had been given her and her husband respecting the eating of the fruit of a particular tree, insinuating at the same time that it was very improbable that God should impose upon them such an unnecessary restraint. Then, on being informed that the tasting of that fruit was forbidden, and that the penalty of death was to be influenced on them in the event of their disobedience, he intimated that such a consequence could never follow; that, on the contrary, the benefits which should arise to them from eating of that fruit were incalculable. In this manner he led her on, from parleying with him, to give him credit; and, from believing him, to compelling with his solicitations. And thus it is that he acts towards us. He, for a time, conceals his full purpose. He pleads at first for nothing more than the gratification of the eye, the ear, the imagination; but is no sooner master of one fort, or station, than he plants his artillery there, and renews his assaults, till the whole soul has surrendered to his dominion.

THE OTHER GRAND DEVICE IS TO KEEP MEN FROM GOD

If, after having yielded to his suggestions, the soul were to return to God with penitence and contrition, all Satan's wiles, however successful they had been before, would be frustrated at once. The next labor therefore of our great adversary is to secure his captive, so he may not escape out of his hands. The wiles he makes use of to accomplish this come next under our consideration.

He will begin with misrepresenting to his captives their own character. While he will insinuate that, though they may have transgressed in some smaller matters, yet they have never committed any great sin, and therefore have no

42

need to disquiet themselves with apprehensions of God's wrath. If he cannot compose their minds in that way, he will suggest, that their iniquities have been so numerous, and so heinous, as to preclude all hope of forgiveness. He will endeavor to make them believe that they have been guilty of the unpardonable sin, or that their day of grace is past; so that they may as well take their fill of present delights, since all attempts to secure eternal happiness will be fruitless. To such artifices as these our Lord refers, when he tells us, that the strong man armed keeps his palace and his goods in peace.

Next he will misrepresent to his captives the character of God. He will impress them with the idea that God is too merciful to punish anyone eternally for such trifling faults as theirs. Or, if that fails, to lull them asleep he will intimate that the insulted majesty of heaven demands vengeance; that the justice and holiness of Deity would be dishonored if pardon were vouchsafed to such offenders as they. Probably too, he will suggest that God has not elected them and that, therefore, they must perish since they cannot alter his decrees or save themselves without His aid. He will, as in his assaults upon our blessed Lord, bring the scriptures themselves to countenance his lies. And, by a misapplication of difficult and detached passages, endeavor to hide from us the perfections of our God as harmonizing and glorified in our redemption. It was in this matter that he strove to discourage Joshua and to detain David in his bonds. Such advantage too he sought to take of the incestuous Corinthian. If this stratagem is not defeated he will prevail over us to our eternal ruin.

But there is another stratagem which, for the subtlety of its texture, the frequency of its use, and the high degree of its success in destroying souls, deserves more especial notice. When effectual resistance has been made to the foregoing temptations, and, in spite of all these misrepresentations, the sinner has attained a just view both of his own character and of God's, then Satan has recourse to another wile that promises indeed to the believer a speedy growth in the divine life, but is intended really to divert him from all proper thoughts both of himself and of God.

He will *"Transform himself into an angel of light"* (2 Corinthians 11:14)

He will make use of some popular minister, or some talkative church member, as his agent in this business. He will by means of his emissaries draw the young convert to matters of doubtful disputation. He will perplex his mind with some intricate questions respecting matters of doctrine, or of discipline in the church. He will either controvert and explode acknowledged truths, or carry them to an extreme, turning spirituality to mysticism or liberty to licentiousness. Having entangled him in this snare, he will puff him up with a conceit of his own superior attainments and speedily turn him from the simplicity that is in Christ. Little do his agents, who appear to be "ministers of righteousness' imagine that they are really ministers of the devil. Also little do they who are persuaded by them, consider "In what a snare they are taken". God himself, who sees all these secret transactions, and discerns their fatal tendency, has given us this very account and thereby guarded us against this dangerous device. Satan originates false doctrine to mislead mankind. The Bible says:

The Spirit clearly says that in latter times some

44

will abandon the faith and follow deceiving spir-
its and things taught by demons.

(1 Timothy 4:1)

Satan encourages all doctrine that is contrary to the scriptures because it detracts from Jesus Christ. If he can get you side tracked on doctrine...taking your mind from the redemption through Christ...then he can lead you astray.

Thus have we seen the temptations, by which Satan leads men into sin, together with the seasons, the mean, and the manner, of his assaults. We have seen also how he keeps men from God, even by misrepresenting to them their own character and God's, or by diverting them from due attention either to themselves or God.

Let us now proceed, in the second place, to point out the means by which these wiles may be defeated.

This part of our subject will come again into discussion, both generally, in the next discourse, and particularly, when we teach of the various pieces of armor provided for us. Nevertheless, we must distinctly, though briefly, show in this place:

- What we are to understand by the whole armor of God

- How we are to put it on

- In what way it will enable us to withstand the devils wiles

Armor is of two kinds: defensive and offensive; the one to protect ourselves; the other to assail our enemy. God has provided for us everything that is necessary for a successful

45

maintenance of the Christian warfare. Is our head exposed to the assaults of Satan? There is "A HELMET" to guard it. Is our heart liable to be pierced? There is a 'BREAST-PLATE' to defend it. Are our feet subject to such wounds as may cause us to fall? There are 'SHOES' or greaves, for their protection. Is our armor likely to be loosened? There is a 'GIRDLE' to keep it fast. Are there apertures, by which a well aimed dart may finds entrance? There is a "SHIELD" which may be moved for the defense of every part, as occasion may require. Lastly, the Christian soldier is furnished with a sword also, by the skilful use of which he may inflict deadly wounds to his adversary.

But here it will be asked; "How shall we get this armor, and how shall we put it on?" To obtain it, we must go to the armory of heaven and receive it from the hands of the Captain of our salvation. No creature in the universe can give it to us. He, and he only, who formed it, can impart it to us. As when God had decreed the destruction of Babylon, we are told that:

> *The Lord opened his armory, and brought forth the weapons of his indignation.*
> (Jeremiah 50:25)

So, when he commissioned us to go forth against sin and Satan, he must supply us with arms, whereby alone we can execute his will. We must daily go to him in prayer, that he would furnish us from head to foot, or rather, that he himself would be "our shield and buckler" our almighty protector and deliverer.

When we have received our armor, then we are to "put it on". It is not given us to look at, but to use. Not to wear for our amusement, but to gird on for actual service. We must examine it, to see that it is indeed of celestial temper, and that no part is wanting. We must adjust it carefully in all its parts, that it may not be cumbersome and useless in the hour of need. And, when we have clothed ourselves with it, then we must put forth our strength, and use it for the purposes for which it is designed.

Our more particular directions must be reserved till we consider the use of each distinct part of this armor. At present, we shall only add that, if we thus go forth to the combat, we shall surely vanquish our subtle enemy. We say not that he will never wound us, for the most watchful of us are sometimes off our guard and the most experienced of us are sometimes deceived. But, we can assure the whole army of Christians that Satan shall never prevail against them. Their head shall be preserved from error, their heart from iniquity, and their feet from falling.

What remains then but that we call on all of you to put on this armor? Let not any imagine that they can stand without it; for, if Adam was vanquished even in paradise, how much more shall we be overpowered? If the perfect armor with which he was clad by nature proved insufficient for the combat, how shall we stand, who are altogether stripped of every defense? If Satan, while yet a novice in the art of tempting, "beguiled our first parents by this subtlety," how much more will he beguile and ruin us after so many years of additional experience? Arise then, all of you, and gird yourselves for the combat.

> *Ye careless ones, know that you are already led captive by the devil at his will.*
>
> (2 Timothy 2:26)

And the more you think yourselves secure, the more you show that you are the dupes of Satan's wiles.

Ye weak and timid, be strong, fear not; hath not God commanded you? Be strong and of good courage; Be not afraid, neither be dismayed; For the Lord your God is with you, whithersoever ye go.

(Joshua 1:9)

Only go forth in dependence upon God, and no weapon that is formed against you shall ever prosper.

(Isaiah 54:17)

But take care that you have on the whole armor of God. In vain will be the use of any, if the whole is not used. One part left unprotected will prove as fatal as if you were exposed in every part. But, if you follow this counsel, you may defy all the hosts of hell. For,

The weakest of you shall be as David, and the house of David shall be as God.

(Zechariah 12:8)

CHAPTER FOUR

To Withstand the Power of Satan

For we wrestle not against flesh and blood, but against principalities in high places. Wherefore take unto you the whole armor of God, that you may be able to withstand in the evil day, and having done all, to stand.

(Ephesians 6: 12,13)

In persuading men to undertake any arduous office, and more especially to enlist into the army, it is customary to keep out of view, as much as possible, the difficulties and dangers they will be exposed to, and to allure them by prospects of pleasure, or honor. It was far otherwise with Christ and his apostles. When our Lord invited men to enlist under his banners, he told them that they would have to enter on a course of pain and self-denial.

If any man will be my disciple, let him deny him-self, and take up his cross daily, and follow me.

49

(Luke 9:23)

Thus Paul, at the very time that he is endeavoring to recruit the Christian army, tells us plainly, that the enemies we shall have to combat are the most subtle and powerful of any in the universe. Deceit and violence, the two great engines of cruelty and oppression, are their daily practice and delight.

In conformity with the apostle's plan, we have opened to you, in some small measure, the wiles of that adversary whom we are prompting you to oppose: and we will now proceed to set before you somewhat of his power; still however encouraging you not to be dismayed, but to go forth against him with an assurance of victory.

We will show you:

What a powerful adversary we have to contend with.

As soon as any man enlists under the banner of Christ, the world will turn against him, even as the kings of Canaan did against the Gibeonites the very instant they had made a league with Joshua.

Those of his own household will most probably be his greatest foes.

(Matthew 10:36)

To oppose these manfully is no easy task: but yet these are of no consideration in comparison of our other enemies. "We wrestle not against flesh and blood", says the apostle, "But against all the principalities and powers" of hell. It is not merely in a rhetorical way that the apostle accumulates so many expressions to designate our enemies. The different terms he uses are well calculated to exhibit their power;

which will appear to us great in deed, if we consider what he intimates respecting their nature, their number, and their office.

With respect to their nature, they are "wicked spirits." Once they were bright angels around the throne of God; but

"They kept not their first estate", and therefore they were *"cast down to hell"* (Jude 1:6, 2 Peter 2:4).

Though they have lost the holiness, they still retain the power of angels. As angels, they excel in strength, and are far greater in power and might than any human being. Thy have, moreover, an immense advantage over us, in that they are spirits. Were they flesh and blood like ourselves, we might see them approaching, and either flee from them, or fortify ourselves against them. At least, there would be some time when, through weariness, they must intermit their efforts. But, being spirits, their approaches to us are invisible and incessant.

Their number is also intimated, in that they are represented as "principalities and powers," consisting of multitudes who hold, like men on earth and angels in heaven, various degrees of honor and authority under one head. To form a conjecture respecting their numbers would be absurd, since we are totally in the dark on that subject. This however we know, that they are exceeding many. Our Lord cast no less than seven out of one woman; and one man was possessed by a whole troop or "legion' at once. (Luke 8:2; Mark 5:9)

We have reason therefore to think that their number far exceeds that of the human species; because there is no human being beyond the reach of their assaults, no, not for a single hour. Nor are they formidable merely on account of their number, but principally on account of their union, and subordination under one leader. We read of *"the devil and his angels"* (Matthew 25:41), as a king and his subjects. Though we know not what precise ranks and orders there may be among them, we know the name of their chief, even "Beelzebub, the prince of the devils." It is because of their acting thus in concert with one another, that they are so often spoken of as one; and, well they may be, for the whole, multitude of them are so perfectly one in operation and design, that, if one spy out an advantage, he may in an instant have a legion more to second his endeavors. As this constitutes the strength of armies on earth, so does it give tenfold power to our spiritual enemies.

The office which they execute as "the rulers of this dark world" may serve yet further to give us an idea of their strength. It is true; this office was not delegated to them, but usurped by them. Still, however, they retain it by God's permission and exercise it to our cost. Satan is expressly called:

> *...the prince of this world...the god of this world...the prince of the power of the air, the spirit that now worketh in the children of disobedience...*
>
> (John 14:30; 2 Corinthians 4:4; Ephesians 2:2)

He *"blinds them"* (2 Kings 6:18).

Thus blinded by Satan so they may not see, then just as the prophet led the Syrians, he leads them whithersoever he will. He takes them captive altogether. A few indeed who are brought out of darkness into the marvelous light of the gospel, have cast off his yoke. But, except them, the whole world, enveloped in worse than Egyptian darkness, lies under him as its' universal monarch. The very elements are under his control, and concur with men and devils to fulfill his will. Would he deprive Job of his substance? Hosts of Sabeans and Chaldeans come at his call to plunder him. Would he destroy all his family? The wind rises at his command to smite their house, and overwhelm them in its ruins. (Job 1)

Such are the enemies with whom we have to contend. If we desire to pursue earthly things, we can go on with ease. We can follow them without interruption from day to day, and from year to year. With respect to theses things, the devils would rather help us forward than obstruct our way. But the very instant we begin to seek "heavenly things" all hell is in alarm; just as all the Canaanites were, when they understood that Joshua's spies had been seen in their land. If we begin to listen to the Word of God, Satan will send some emissary, some child of his, whom he has endued to peculiar subtlety, to turn us from the faith. If the Word, like a good seed, is sown upon our hearts, he will send a host of devils, like birds of the air, to pick up the seed. If any, in spite of his efforts, take root in our hearts, he will instantly sow tares to grow up with the wheat, and thorns to choke it. We cannot go into the presence of God to pray.

Satan will be at our right hand to resist us.
(Zechariah 3:1)

The conflict we have to maintain with him is not like that which is common to our armies, where a part bear the brunt of the battle, and the rest are reserved for back-up. In this view it is more properly compared to "a wrestling" where every man meets his antagonist, and must continue the contest, till the fall of one party decides the victory. Such the scripture describes our contest to be. As such it is proved to be by every man's experience. Any man who will only observe the ease with which he enters upon his worldly calling, and keeps up his attention to it, and the comparative difficulty he finds as soon as ever he addresses himself to the concerns of his soul, will see that there is in him an impotence and reluctance, for which he cannot account, unless he acknowledge, what the scripture so fully warns him of, a satanic agency.

But, shall we be intimidated on this account, and induced to surrender ourselves to Satan without a conflict? No! Formidable as he is, there is one above him, who circumscribes his powers, and limits his operations. He did, by God's permission, 'cast' some of the church of Smyrna into prison, that they might be tried for ten days. If he could have accomplished all that was in his heart, he would have cast them all into hell that they might perish forever. So far from being irresistible, he may be resisted. Yes, and vanquished too, by the weakest of God's saints.

To encourage you therefore to fight against him, we shall show:

How We May Effectually Withstand Him

The apostle renews, though with some variation, the directions he gave before;

> *Not thinking it grievous to himself to repeat any thing that may conduce to our safety.*
> (Philippians 3:1)

54

Peter also was,

...careful to put Christians frequently in remembrance of many things, notwithstanding they knew them, and were established in the present truth.

(2 Peter 1:12)

Therefore, may we call your attention once more to the exhortation in the text.

Indeed, if the putting on of the whole armor of God was necessary to guard against the wiles of the devil, it cannot be less necessary as a preservative against his power. The exhortation enforced by this new consideration cannot reasonably be thought an uninteresting repetition.

We shall have no need to repeat any former observations, seeing that what is new in the exhortation will afford abundant matter for profitable and seasonable remark.

The time mentioned in the test as 'the evil day', refers to those particular periods when Satan makes his most desperate attacks. Sometimes he retires from us for a season, as he did from our Lord; or, at least, gives us somewhat of a respite from any violent assaults. But, he watches his opportunity to renew his efforts, when by bringing a host of devils to his aid, or finding us off our guard, he may exert his power to more effect. Such a season was that wherein David complained that,

...his enemies, compassing him like bees, thrust sore at him that he might fall.

(Psalm 118:10-13)

The Lord Jesus Christ, himself, was so weakened by him as to need an angel from heaven to administer strength and consolation (Luke 22:43).

All who know any thing about 'Satan's devices' must have noticed this in their own experience. There have been times when the enemy appeared unmindful of his work, and other times when,

> *...he has come in like a flood. So, if the Spirit of the Lord had not lifted up a standard against him.*
> (Isaiah 59:19)

He must have utterly overwhelmed them. The hour of death is a season when he usually puts forth all his power,

> *...having great wrath because his time is so short.*
> (Revelation 12:12)

Now, what shall we do in such seasons, if not clad in the whole armor of God? What hope can we have of withstanding such an enemy? If he should find us armed, would he not sift us as wheat, and reduce us to mere chaff? Would he not scatter us as smoke out of the chimney, or chaff driven by a whirlwind? Would he not precipitate thousands of us, as he did the swine, into instantaneous destruction, and into the abyss of hell?

But, if we are armed with the divine armor, we need not fear. He can have no power against us any further than it is given him from above.

> *Howbeit he meaneth not so, neither doth his heart think so.*
> (Isaiah 10:7)

His efforts against us shall ultimately conduce to our good, to make us more humble, more vigilant and, more expert.

This is particularly intimated in the text. In this the encouragement given to us exceeds what was contained in the former exhortation. There, we were taught to expect that we will not be vanquished by our subtle enemy. Here, we are encouraged with an assurance that we shall not only effectually withstand his efforts, even when they are most desperate, but shall "stand" as victors on the field of battle, after having put our enemies to flight. To this also agree the words of James.

...resist the devil, and he shall flee from you.
(James 4:7)

He shall not overcome you, but shall be so intimidated by your prowess as to flee from you with the greatest appreciation. Blessed Truth! This mighty fiend who dared to enter the lists with an archangel, and to contend even with the Son of God himself, shall be so terrified at the sight of a Christian champion, as now only to "forbear touching him,' but even to flee from his presence as for his very life.

It is true, Satan will never finally give over the contest, till we are entirely beyond his reach; nor, at any time is he so vanquished or intimidated that he would not raise another host, like that which was defeated, and renew his attack upon us. His malice shall terminate in his own confusion. He may succeed in bruising our heel, but we shall ultimately bruise his head. Our weapons, through God, will be mighty, even when wielded by the feeblest arm. We shall go on "conquering and to conquer" till we set our feet upon his neck, and return with triumphant exultation from the combat, saying:

> *Lord, even the devils are subject unto us through Thy name.*
>
> (Luke 10:17)

This is not your greatest encouragement. For as soon as you have 'done all' that God has designed for you in this state of warfare, you shall 'stand' before God, united to that noble army that are now enjoying their triumphs in His presence. Having,

> *...fought the good fight and finished your course, there shall be given to you a crown of righteousness and glory.*
>
> (2 Timothy 4:7-8)

You shall bear the palm of victory in the courts of heaven. Then it shall be fulfilled to you what was spoken by our Lord,

> *To him that overcometh will I give to sit with me upon my throne, even as I also overcame, and am set down with my father upon His throne.*
>
> (Revelation 3:21)

> *...only be thou faithful unto death; and God will give thee a crown of life.*
>
> (Revelation 2:10)

Before we dismiss this subject, we would address a few words.

To those who have never yet wrestled with this great adversary. We hope you are now convinced that it is not a needless labor to engage in this contest. However, you may still be induced to decline it, from the idea that it is a hopeless work. Know this, that you have undertaken a task which is infinitely more difficult than this. While you refuse to wrestle with Satan, you are actually wrestling with God himself. He, who infallibly discerns and rightly estimates your conduct, says that "Ye resist the Holy Ghost" and "contend with your Maker". Your consciences will inform you that you have often "fought against God" by resisting the influence of His word and spirit. Suppose then you gain the victory. Suppose God gives up the contest and says "My spirit shall strive with him no longer". What will you have to boast of? What cause will you have for joy? Awful will be that day wherein God shall say,

> *Let him alone.*

> (Hosea 4:17)

From that hour your condemnation will be sure, and Satan will have perfectly gained his point. Judge then whether it is better to contend with Satan than with God; with him whom you are sure to conquer, to your eternal happiness, than with Him by whose avenging arm you must choose for your enemy, God or Satan. May God incline you to enlist under the Redeemer's banner and in His strength to combat all the enemies of your salvation.

Let us speak to those who have begun the arduous contest. Be not afraid of your great adversary. Do not be like the unbelieving Israelites, who, because the Anakim were of such extraordinary stature, and dwelt in cities that were walled up to heaven, were afraid to go up against them. Rather say, with Caleb,

> *...they shall be bread for us.*

> (Numbers 14:1-9)

Instead of destroying, they shall be an occasion of good to our souls. Their spoils shall enrich us. The opposition that they make shall only be the means of displaying more abundantly the love and faithfulness of our God. 'Take unto you' again and again the 'whole armor of God'; and fight, not as one that 'beateth the air', but as one determined to conquer or die. If at any time you are tempted to give up the contest, think of,

> *...those who (now) through faith and patience inherit the promises.*
>
> (Hebrews 6:12)

Once they were conflicting like you. But, now they rest from their labors, and are spectators of your conflicts. It is but a little time, and you also shall be numbered with them.

> *Greater is He that is you, than he that is in the world.*
>
> (1 John 4:4)

So, go forth in the name of Christ; and His triumphs shall be the pattern, the pledge, the earnest of your own.

CHAPTER FIVE

The Christian's Girdle

Stand therefore, having your loins girt about with truth.

(Ephesians 6:14)

The first part of armor mentioned is the "Girdle of Truth".

Stand therefore, having your loins girt about with Truth.

(vs. 14)

Concerning "Truth", Jesus Christ said,

I am the way, the truth, and the life.

(John 14:6)

Since Jesus Christ is the personification of truth, to put on the girdle of truth is to,

Put...On the Lord Jesus Christ.

(Romans 13:14)

Because He is God, Jesus Christ is the embodiment of all truth.

Not only is Jesus Christ the Truth, but the Word of God is also Truth. Concerning His own, Jesus asked the Father,

> *...sanctify them through thy truth. Thy Word is Truth.*
>
> (John 17:17)

Christ is the living Word and the Bible is the written Word, and these together form the believer's girdle of truth.

If we want to be protected against the attacks of the evil one, we must know Jesus Christ as our savior and be faithful students of the Word of God. The written word directs our attention to the Living Word. The better we really know the scriptures, the more we will want to please God in everything we do.

The Psalmist said,

> *Thy word have I hid in mine heart, that I might not sin against thee.*
>
> (Psalm 119:11)

This shows us the effect of the word in a believer's life.

> *...for the word of God is quick* (living), *and powerful and sharper than any two edged sword, piercing even to the dividing asunder of soul and spirit, and of the joints and marrow, and is a discerner of the thoughts and intents of the heart.*
>
> (Hebrews 4:12)

To have our *"loins girt about with truth"* is to have the living and the written Word controlling our lives. The believer who loves the truth and lives it will have a strong spiritual life. Such a person will not be,

...carried about with every wind of doctrine, by the sleight of men, and cunning craftiness, whereby they lie in wait to deceive.

(Ephesians 4:14)

As you study the scriptures regarding warfare, they act as a honing blade to sharpen your sword.

The first Truth the apostle mentions is "TRUTH". In elucidating we will show,

What we are to understand by "Truth"

Its use and office in the Christian warfare

I. What are we to understand by "Truth"?

It is a term of extensive signification. It is sometimes put for the gospel; in which sense the apostle speaks of:

...obeying the truth.

(1 Peter 1:22)

In this place it rather means sincerely. The two terms are often used together as synonymous expressions. In Joshua's farewell discourse, he says:

...serve the Lord in sincerity and truth.

(Joshua 24:14)

Paul exhorts us to:

...keep the feast with the unleavened bread of sincerity and truth.

(1 Corinthians 5:8)

But sincerity, Christian sincerity, is very little understood. For the most part, it is considered as importing nothing more than a good intention, without any reference to the manner in which that good intention operates. But the sincerity of which the text speaks is a Christian "Grace", and, consequently, it must include something widely different from that which may be exercised by superstitious bigots.

To mark it as distinctly as possible, we shall notice four things that are implied in it:

First: It implies a desire and intention to please God. There is one canon, one universal rule of action, prescribed to us in the scriptures; namely, that,

> *...whether we eat or drink, or whatever we do, we should do all to the glory of God.*
> (1 Corinthians 10:31)

Therefore, whatever springs from other motives and principles must argue a lack of sincerity, in proportion as God's honor is superceded by any selfish considerations. When Jehu, in compliance with God's command to destroy the family of Ahab, his obedience was not considered as sincere, because he was actuated rather by vain glory than by a real desire to please God; and the blood that he shed in executing the divine command was on that very account avenged by God himself upon his posterity. (2 Kings 9 & 10)

The Jews also complied with the institutions of Moses in observing their religious fasts and feasts. However, because they fasted and feasted unto themselves rather than unto God, and sought rather to cover their own enormities by such observances than really to honor God, their services were deemed hypocritical, and were rejected with abhorrence. Thus must all our duties, civil or religious, have respect to God. We must have a "single eye" if we would please Him. If we bring forth fruit to ourselves only, we are 'empty *vines*' (Hosea 10:1). We are unprofitable servants.

Second: <u>Sincerity implies a serving of God according to the light we enjoy.</u>

Sincerity will doubtless consist with defective views both of Christian duty and Christian liberty. It will not consist with allowed deviations from an acknowledged duty, either in a way of omission or of commission.

> *...the wisdom that is from above is without partiality and without hypocrisy.*
> (James 3:17)

To be,

> *...partial in the law...*
> (Malachi 2:9)

is to dissemble with God. Whether we make outward duties a cloak for inward lusts, or present to God a mere,

> *...form of godliness without the power of it...*
> (1 Timothy 3:5)

we are really,

> *...hypocrites in heart...*
> (Job 36:13)

and therefore can have no pretensions to sincerity.

Third: <u>Sincerity requires a desire to know the will of God more perfectly.</u>

Here it is that many, who have appeared most sincere, have failed. Paul before his conversion,

...thought he ought to do many things contrary to the name of Jesus.

(Acts 26:9)

He truly did them with a zeal suited to his persuasion. But can it be said that at that time he possessed the Christian virtue of sincerity? By no means; he had opportunities enough of information. The writings of Moses and the prophets were plain enough to convince any man that was not blinded by prejudice and carried away by his own impetuous passions. Besides, he might have gone to the fountain head, and enquired of Jesus himself, what grounds there were for believing him to be the messiah. Above all, he lived when the gospel was preached in all its purity, and attested from heaven by miracles without number. Why then did he not set himself to enquire more candidly? Why did he not, like the Bereans, search the scripture, to see if things were as the apostles declared them to be? (Acts 17:11) This would not agree with his infuriated zeal. He hated the light, and therefore sought to the uttermost to extinguish it.

How different was the conduct of Nathanael. He participated in the prejudices of his countrymen, and hastily concluded that:

...no good thing could come out of Nazareth.

(John 1:46)

But when he was desired to 'come and see' for himself, he availed himself of the opportunity to form his judgment on surer grounds. On the very first demonstration which our Lord gave of His Messiahship, Nathanael believed in Jesus; thereby, evidenced his right to that title which our Lord had given him.

66

...an Israelite indeed, in whom there is no guile.
(John 1:47)

Fourth: <u>Sincerity requires a determination to serve God without any regard to consequences.</u>

Our duty to God is paramount to every other consideration. When we know what he requires of us, we are not to be diverted from it by any losses or any sufferings. Who does not see the insincerity of those who believed in Christ, but were afraid to confess him; and of that amiable youth who turned back from Christ rather than part with his possessions? (John 12:42 & Matthew 19:22) If we are truly upright in heart, we will say as Paul when he was solicited to shun the trials and afflictions which, as the spirit testified, awaited him in every city,

> *I am ready not only to be bound, but also to die at Jerusalem for the name of the Lord Jesus.*
> (Acts 21:31)

> *...and if the trials be ever so severe, we shall still hold fast our integrity...none of these things move me, neither count I my life dear unto myself, so that I may finish my course with joy, and fulfill my duty to God.*
> (Acts 20:24)

This representation of truth is both illustrated and confirmed by the conduct of Paul on the occasion of his conversion to God. Till that hour he had been walking blindly "after the course of this world', and 'in the way of his own heart'; but as soon as his eyes were opened, even before he had any clear knowledge of Christianity, he desired to know, and determined to execute, the whole will of God.

Lord, what wilt thou have me to do? Thou needest only to show me wherein I am wrong, and to teach me thy way, and I will instantly, through thy assistance, change my conduct, and devote myself to thy service; nor shall any considerations of hope or fear ever turn me from the path prescribed by thee. Nor was this a vain boast.

(Acts 9:6)

...for he conferred not with flesh and blood, but set himself without delay to 'preach the faith' which he had labored to destroy, and persisted in preaching it even unto death.

(Galatians 1:15-24)

II. The nature of truth being thus ascertained let us proceed to show –its use and office in the Christian warfare.

Among the various parts of a soldier's armor a girdle was of principal importance. In this view it is frequently mentioned in the Holy Scriptures. The prophet, describing the irresistible fury with which the Chaldeans should over-run Palestine, says,

...none shall be weary or stumble among them, none shall slumber nor sleep; neither shall the girdle of their loins be loosed.

(Isaiah 5:27)

Our blessed Lord, who, as the captain of our salvation, was arrayed like all the soldiers of his army, is represented by the same prophet as habited in this manner,

...righteousness shall be the girdle of His loins, and faithfulness the girdle of His reins.

(Isaiah 11:5)

68

The use of the girdle was to keep the armor compact, and to strengthen the loins. These are the offices which 'Truth' performs for the Christian soldier.

In the first place, it compacts all the graces with which his soul is armed. As the different parts of armor with which the body is fortified would hang loose, and leave many apertures through which a wound might be inflicted, if they were not fastened together by a belt or girdle, as would the Christian's graces prove insufficient for his defense if they were not all compacted together by the girdle of sincerity. Let us look at persons that seemed armed from head to foot, and prepared to defy all the powers of darkness. See Johanan and the remnant of the Jews whom the Chaldeans had not taken in captivity, coming to the prophet, entreating him to ask counsel for them from God, and vowing in the most solemn manner to comply with any direction which the Lord should give them by His mouth. We have not a more hopeful appearance in all the sacred records. But, they dissembled with God. No sooner was the answer given them, than they showed by their conduct that they were not sincere in their overtures, and they became the victims of their own hypocrisy. How often are similar failures found amongst ourselves from the very same cause! How many appear penitent and determined to serve their God while they are under some heavy calamity, or in the near prospect of death, and yet reveal their hypocrisy as soon as ever their professions are brought to the test! Yet, daily is that account of the Jews realized amongst us.

When he slew them, then they sought Him, and enquired early after God, and remembered that God was their rock, and the high God their redeemer. Nevertheless, they did but flatter Him with their mouth, and lie unto Him with their tongues. For their heart was not right with Him, neither were they steadfast in His covenant.

(Psalms 78:34-37)

On the other hand, how impenetrable to the darts of the adversary were the graces of those who were sincere before God! Daniel not only would not relinquish, but would not so much as abate or conceal his devotions though menaced with a cruel and speedy death. Nor would the Hebrew youths comply with the edict of a haughty monarch, though they saw a furnace heated for their destruction, and might have pleaded in their defense the example of a whole nation. Thus shall we also be enabled to brave every danger, and to endure death in its most awful forms, if our hearts are upright before God. As all our graces will be compacted together by sincerity, so every distinct grace will derive from it tenfold solidity and strength. Let our 'faith be unfeigned' our 'love without dissimulation', and our spirit altogether 'without guile', and we need fear no assault, however artful, however violent.

Next: The other office of truth is, to strengthen our soul under great and long-continued conflicts.

This particular use of the girdle is repeatedly mentioned by the Psalmist. In reference to himself he says,

...thou hast girded me with strength unto the battle.

(2 Samuel 22:40)

In reference to the Messiah also he uses a similar expression.

The Lord reigneth; He is clothed with majesty.

70

The Lord is clothed with strength, wherewith He hath girded himself.

(Psalm 93:1)

Those who have a divided heart will assuredly be found faulty at the last (Hosea 10:2.)

Numberless are the instances wherein persons who have fought well for a season have fainted at last through this sad defect. But, we will mention only two. In one example, we will see the individual's failure nearly terminated in the destruction of many. The second example, involved one of the most eminent of professed Christians in utter and everlasting ruin. For the former instance we will refer you, not to a man professedly ungodly, nor to a mere novice in religion, but to the most distinguished of the apostles. With the name of Peter we associate the idea of courage undaunted and of piety irreproachable. But, behold him on one occasion, when his loins were loosed, and the girdle was wanting to complete his armor. This valiant hero, who had acquitted himself so nobly in many battles, was at last, through fear of offending the Judaizing Christians, guilty of the basest dissimulation. Peter undermined, by his influence, the most essential doctrine of that gospel which he was sent to preach. By his example, he was able to draw in Barnabas also, and a multitude of others, into the most fatal error. If Paul had not openly rebuked him before all the church, and thereby counteracted the effect of his misconduct, it is not possible to say how far his error might have affected the eternal interest of millions. (Galatians 2)

In the other instance, we must turn our eyes to one whose eminence drew from Paul himself repeated commendations, even such as were bestowed on the evangelist Luke. (Colossians 4:14 & Philemon 24) After years of manly toil and continued danger, Demas was left to prove how weak the strongest are without sincerity. Wearied with his conflicts, he sought repose in the bosom of the world. When if he had fought with more sincerity, he might have endured to the end, and triumphed over all his adversaries. Unhappy man, to retain one secret lust which, like a canker, ate out his vitals, or, like a leak unnoticed, sunk the vessel wherein he was embarked. (2 Timothy 4:10) But, thus it will be with all whose loins are not girt about with truth.

> *...a double minded man will be unstable in all his ways.*
>
> (James 1:8)

But if we have melancholy instances of failure through the want of this virtue, we have many noble instances of persevering zeal in others, whose hearts were right with God. Look at the patriarch's journeying for years in a strange land, when,

> *...they had opportunities enough of returning to their native country' if they had been so minded;*
> (Hebrews 11: 13-16)

but they were sincere in,

> *...seeking out a better country, that is, a heavenly,*

and therefore they lived willingly as,

> *...strangers and pilgrims on the earth.*

Also look at the noble army of martyrs, who,

> *...out of weakness were made strong, waxed*

valiant in fight, and turned to flight the armies of the aliens.

(Hebrews 11: 34-35)

Women also, who, notwithstanding their natural weakness and timidity, would,

...not accept deliverance (from the tortures) *that they might obtain a better resurrection*

Indeed, where is there one who is truly upright before God, who has not frequently evidenced a strength and steadfastness superior to the efforts of unassisted nature? Who has not been called to make many sacrifices pleasure, honor, interest, and to lead a life of continual self-denial, both in the mortifying of inward lusts, and the enduring of outward persecutions? But, *'having set his hand to the plow'* the Christian will not look back; and having put on his armor, he will not put it off but with his life.

The vast importance of truth and sincerity being made apparent let the following advice be duly weighed.

1. Let us enquire whether we possess this part of the Christian armor.

Perhaps there is scarcely anyone who does not fancy his or her self sincere. We can appeal to God that our daily aim is to please Him. Do we desire pleasing God not only in preference to ourselves or others, but in direct opposition to the whole world? Do we labor to approve ourselves to Him, shunning every sinful thing, and doing everything we know to be right? Do we search the scriptures daily, and attend on the ministration of God's Word, on purpose that we may have our sentiments and conduct more entirely conformed to the will of God? Finally, do we disregard the scoffs of an ungodly world and determine to sacrifice even life itself rather than violate the dictates of our conscience? This is sincerity. This is truth. Doubtless there are infirmities in the best of men, and consequently there will be occasional deviations from the path of duty. However, if we be sincere, we shall not allow any sin whatsoever. We shall endeavor to be pure as God is pure and perfect.

O that there were in all of us such a heart as this.
(1 John 3:3)

2. Let us be on our guard against those devices whereby Satan would weaken our sincerity or rob us of the comfort of it.

Satan will put forth all his wiles, and exert all his power, to loosen this girdle. He well knows that if he succeeds in this point all the rest will be easy. Until he can do that, we are invulnerable. He will cover his endeavors with the most specious pretexts and present his temptations in the most alluring shapes. Let us watch against him! Let not the example of an apostle, or the preaching of an angel, lead us to renounce one single truth, or to transgress one single precept. If we are not continually on our guard, that serpent will beguile us. Yes, in spite of all our watchfulness he will deceive us if we are not preserved by God himself. Let us therefore,

...watch and pray that we enter not into temptation.
(Luke 22:46)

If Satan cannot entice us to lay aside our girdle, he will endeavor to deprive us of the comfort of it. He will take occasion from our remaining infirmities to make us think we are a hypocrite and thus he will seek to affect that, through despondency, which he could not affect through any other temptations. Let it then be our daily course to fasten this girdle around our loins so that we may have in ourselves, and give to all around us, indisputable evidence that we both possess and gain by it. Then we can:

> ...*rejoice in the testimony of our conscience that in simplicity and godly sincerity we have our conversation in the world.*
>
> (2 Corinthians 1:12)

Lastly, let us stand thus armed and be in constant readiness to oppose our enemy. Do not fear him but resist him strongly. If we fight we have nothing to fear. It is only when we turn our back that we are left exposed to any mortal injury. In every other part we are armed sufficiently for our defense. Let us then beg of God to put,

> ...*truth in our inward parts.*
>
> (Psalm 51:6)

Let us,

> ...*add to our faith, virtue, knowledge, temperance, patience, godliness, brotherly-kindness, and charity...*
>
> (1 Peter 5-10)

and keep them all compact with the girdle of truth. Then we will have God's promise that,

> ... *we shall never fall.*
>
> (Psalm 25:21)

Through His grace our,

> ... *integrity and uprightness shall preserve us.*

Let us therefore,

...gird up the loins of our mind, and be sober, and hope to the end.

(1 Peter 1:13 & Philippians 1:10)

Only let us be sincere and we shall,

...be without offence till the day of Christ.

CHAPTER SIX

The Christian's Breastplate

Stand – Having On The Breastplate of Right-
eousness

(Ephesians 6:14)

The second part of the armor referred to was the breast-plate of righteousness. The breastplate was worn by the Roman soldier on the upper part of his body and covered both his front and his back. As such, it provided protection for the vital organs of his body.

To Paul, this literal breastplate represented a spiritual breastplate that each believer should use. This spiritual breastplate is an aspect of Christ's protection for the believer against the schemes of the devil. Just as the literal breastplate protected the soldier's heart, so the spiritual breastplate protects the believer's heart. The scriptures view the heart as the seat of the emotions. Satan attacks the believer's emotions to draw his affections and desires

77

away from Christ to the things of this world. The believer is protected from such attacks only as he, by faith, relies on the righteousness of Christ as his breastplate.

We need to remember that our right standing with God is only because of the righteousness of Jesus Christ. The Bible says,

> *...but of Him are ye in Christ Jesus, who of God is made unto us wisdom, and righteousness, and sanctification, and redemption.*
> (1 Corinthians 1:30)

Righteousness differs from sincerity. Sincerity relates to the aims and motives of a person, but righteousness to his actions and habits. *Righteousness is that in actual attainment which sincerity is in desire and purpose.* As was shown in the preceding chapter, sincerity may be found in blind zealots.

That our standing before God is based on His right-eousness, not ours, is also seen from,

> *...but to him that worketh not, but believeth on Him that justifieth the ungodly, his faith is counted for righteousness.*
> (Romans 4:5)

It is this imputed righteousness of Christ – righteous-ness placed on our account when we receive Him as Sav-ior – that cannot be attacked by Satan. This righteousness alone is "wound-proof". The darts of Satan cannot pierce it because it is the righteousness of Christ placed to our account. Regardless of Satan's accusations against us before God, we need not fear losing our position in Christ because we are accepted by God because of Christ's righteousness, not because of our own. However, we can be sure that Satan will attack us on the basis of our behavior and will tempt us to believe that we have lost our standing with God. But, Satan's attacks will not be effective if we stand by faith on what the written Word says and let it assure us of our position before God.

If we fail in the Christian life – and we will fail at times – our position in Christ does not change. The reason for this is that our position is not based on the good we have done, or even on our obedience. It is based on what Christ has done. It is for this reason that Satan's accusations, although at times well grounded because of our behavior, cannot move us from God's presence because we stand there in Christ's righteousness. Christ is our advocate before the father, and he pleads our case righteously as mentioned in:

> *...my little children, these things write I unto you, that ye sin not. And if any man sin, we have an advocate with the father, Jesus Christ the righteous; and He is the propitiation for our sins. And not for ours only, but also for the sins of the whole world.*

(1 John 2:1-2)

Many believers do not realize that Christ's righteousness is the basis of their security. Those who do not understand this become introspective and discouraged in their Christian life and lay themselves open to Satan's attacks. Satan is always looking for opportunities to attack a believer. When Satan sees one who has sinned and who is greatly depressed because of his sin, Satan will take advantage of that believer and will bring him even further discourage-

Are You Ready for War?

ment. Some become so depressed they even believe they have committed the unpardonable sin, not realizing that the Christian cannot commit such a sin, for all his sins were pardoned when he received Christ as Savior.

We should once and for all put on the breastplate of righteousness. That is, by faith we should relay on our position in Christ. But it is not enough to know the doctrine.

The doctrine must be put into practice.

(Ephesians 4:24) tells us,

> ...and that ye put on the new man, which after God is created in righteousness and true holiness.

We are also told,

> ...for we are His workmanship, created in Christ Jesus unto good works, which God hath before ordained that we should walk in them.
>
> (Ephesians 2:10)

We must not forget that we were created new for the purpose of good works, so those of us who know Christ should do good and bring glory to Him.

One of Satan's master tricks for those who know of their safety in Christ is to cause them to think that they have no obligation to do good. It is not pleasing to the Lord if we live a worldly, indifferent Christian life, and then put our conscience to sleep by saying something like "before God I am righteous in Christ. What else do I need?" Paul's words answer this type of thinking.

> ...what shall we say then? Shall we continue in sin, that grace may abound? God forbid.
>
> (Romans 6:1-2)

80

Since our standing is righteous in Christ, our practice should be right-doing. Christ is our righteousness for salvation, and He is also our life for our daily right living.

Let us be careful about presuming upon the grace of God. If we are not concerned about glorifying Christ in our daily walk, we may force God to set us aside and to severely chasten us to bring us to our spiritual senses. Paul gave instructions to the Corinthian church concerning what to do about an incorrigible individual. Paul said for them:

> *...to deliver such a one unto Satan for the destruction of the flesh, that the spirit may be saved in the day of the Lord Jesus.*
>
> (1 Corinthians 5:5)

Paul also referred to those believers who will not be rewarded when they stand before the Lord.

> *...if any man's work shall be burned, he shall suffer loss; but, he himself shall be saved. Yet so as by fire.*
>
> (1 Corinthians 3:15)

> *...Such an individual, although a believer, has not allowed Christ to work in and through his life so there is no reward for him at the judgment seat of Christ.*
>
> (2 Corinthians 5:10)

So let us put on the breastplate of righteousness both as to our position in Christ and as to our practice in our daily walk, and thereby we will defeat Satan.

There are (2) points to be considered by us:

1. The necessity of righteousness for our defense

2. Its' sufficiency to protect us

THE NECESSITY OF RIGHTEOUSNESS

In order to destroy us, our great adversary uses both deceit and violence. Against both of which it becomes us to be armed in order that we may discover the one and repel the other.

Righteousness then is necessary, in the first place, that we may discover Satan's wiles.

> ...*The God of this world blinds the eyes of them that believe not.*
>
> (2 Corinthians 4:4)

It is astonishing to what a degree he deludes their souls. He instigates them to the commission of sin under the idea that it is at least excusable, if not altogether justifiable and right. He teaches them to,

> ...*call evil good, and good evil. To put darkness for light and light for darkness; bitter for sweet, and sweet for bitter.*
>
> (Isaiah 5:20)

We may see one man carried on by ostentation and vanity while he thinks himself actuated by zeal for God. Another yields to a vindictive spirit, yet supposes that he is only maintaining a just regard for his own character, or perhaps for the rights of the community. Through the agency of that subtle fiend, covetousness assumes the name of prudence; prodigality is nothing but a commendable excess of generosity. The cruelest machinations of bigotry are deemed a service well pleasing to God. Who has not noticed in others this sad infatuation? Who has not seen his neighbors acting under the influence of a bad principle while they were at the same time as strongly persuaded that they were right as if there were no room for doubt?

Thus it is more or less with every unrenewed person. Too often with those also who are yet weak in the faith. They go on *'not knowing what spirit they are of'*. In vain do ministers set forth the evil of such a state. In vain do they discriminate and mark the difference between truth and error. In vain do they endeavor to persuade men in private, as well as in their public ministration. In vain do they confirm every word with the infallible dictates of inspiration. For while men continue destitute of righteousness,

...they have eyes and see not, ears and hear not, neither do they understand.
(Matthew 13:14)

Nothing will effectually show men their error till they are,

...renewed in the spirit of their mind.
(Ephesians 4:23)

Then they have a film removed from their eyes. Then they have a spiritual discernment. They are no longer deceived by specious appearances. They taste and see the real qualities of things. Being,

...brought out of darkness into marvelous light.
(1 Peter 2:9)

They view everything, in a measure, as God himself views it. The greater their proficiency in the divine life, the clearer is their perception of the good or evil that exists. Not in their actions only, but in their motives and principles of action. Hence, it is that the apostle exhorts us to,

...be transformed by the renewing of our minds, that we may prove (and discern, not by theory

83

only, but by actual experiment) *what is that good and acceptable and perfect will of God.*

(Romans 12:2)

Righteousness is further necessary that we may repel the assaults of our enemy.

Sin not only blinds, but debilitates the soul. It is scarcely to be conceived how impotent the natural man is to resist the temptations of Satan. For the most part he makes no resistance at all. But follows the dictates of his imperious master, and yields a willing obedience to his most fatal suggestions. To the ungodly Jews our Lord justly observed,

...ye are of your father the devil, and the lusts of your father ye will do.

(John 8:44)

Sometimes conscience will make a stand against the wicked one; but, soon it is over-powered, and either bribed into consent, or stunned to silence, or forced, in spite of all its' efforts, to give way. It may cause one to tremble; another to reform in many things; another to become almost a Christian; another to make a profession of religion, and openly to join himself to the church of Christ. But Satan has nothing to fear from its exertions, unless it stimulates a man to seek a thorough change of heart. He laughs at the fears of Felix, the reformation of Herod, the acknowledgements of Agrippa, and the professions of Simon Magus (Acts 8:13, 24-26, 28; Mark 6:20). He well knows that, as long as they are unrenewed, they are fast in his chains, and incapable of any effectual exertion.

...Ephraim, though armed, and carrying bows (were so engulfed by sin that they) *turned back in the day of battle.*

(Psalm 78:9)

84

Nor could Israel stand before their enemies while an Achan was in their camp (Joshua 7:8)

So neither can he resist Satan who yields in any thing to the dominion of sin. If once we

...put away a good conscience,

(1 Timothy 1:19)

we shall speedily

...make shipwreck of our faith.

(1 Timothy 1:19)

But let once the tamest of his victims feel the influence of divine grace, and instantly he casts off the yoke under which he had groaned and asserts his liberty. From that moment Satan is constrained to yield to that *"stronger power that has come against him"*, and to relinquish the prey which he can no longer retain.

The necessity of righteousness being thus established let us proceed to consider:

ITS' SUFFICIENCY

The apostle would not have been so urgent in exhorting us to put on the breastplate of righteousness if he had not believed that it would answer all the purposes for which it was designed. That it will protect us, we are well assured. That it will secure to us the victory, there can be no doubt. For it will turn depravity to sanctity, cowardice to courage, and weakness to strength.

First, it turns depravity to sanctity. It is by our inward corruptions that Satan works. He cannot force us to commit sin. He can only present to us such temptations as are suited to our natural desires and suggest such considera- tion to our minds as are likely to procure our compliance with his will. When he came to assault our Lord, he could not prevail because,

> *...he found nothing in him.*
>
> (John 14:30)

That in the smallest degree closed with his suggestion. But when he comes to us he finds in us a predisposition to receive him. If he assaults our heart, there are many secret lusts that are ready to betray us into his hands. He has but to strike a spark, and there is within us combustible mat- ter in abundance that instantly catches fire, and that, if not extinguished by grace, will burn to the lowest hell. But when the soul is endued with righteousness, its' disposi- tions are altogether changed.

> *...old things are passed away, and all things are become new.*
>
> (2 Corinthians 5:17)

We say not indeed that there are no remains of corrup- tion in the soul, for the old nature still continues, and coun- teracts in a measure the operations of the new nature. *"If the flesh lusts against the spirit, the spirit also lusts against the flesh"*, and gains, not indeed without conflicts, the victo- ry over it. Hence the temptations, which would once have been irresistible, are repelled with indignant firmness. As we see in Joseph, who, when repeatedly solicited to commit adultery, replied with horror,

> *...how shall I do this great wickedness, and sin against God?*
>
> (Genesis 39:9)

This then is one way in which righteousness defends the soul. It makes *"sin appear exceeding sinful"*, and holiness to be esteemed as the perfection of bliss. Thus, by weakening the force of temptation, it enables us with success to resist the tempter.

In the next place, it turns cowardice into courage. Satan gets peculiar advantage over men by means of their carnal fears. In whatever degree men are endued with natural fortitude, their courage fails them when they are called to bear the cross of Christ. When our blessed Lord ministered on earth, Nicodemus, though a ruler and governor, was afraid to come in open day lest he should be thought to favor his cause; nor did,

> *...the chief rulers, who believed in Him, dared not to confess Him, because they loved the praise of men more than the praise of God.*
>
> (John 12:42-43)

In instances without number have men, who were able to brave death on the battlefield, shown themselves unable to endure the scorn and contempt that universally attach to religious characters. So true is that declaration of Solomon.

> *...the fear of man bringeth a snare.*
>
> (Proverbs 29:35)

Righteousness emboldens the soul, and enables it to meet the hatred and menaces, or the sneers and ridicule of an ungodly world, with a holy indifference. Yes, it causes the soul to rejoice in these things as tokens for good and as testimonies of the divine favor.

Look at the astonishing change that came over Peter! When he had inconsiderately laid aside his armor, he was intimidated by the voice of a maid-servant and induced to deny his Lord with oaths and curses. But when he had put on his breastplate, he was undismayed in the presence of the whole council of the Jews. He boldly charged upon the rulers that were before him the guilt of murdering their Messiah. When they endeavored to silence him with threats, he undauntedly replied,

> *...whether it be right to hearken unto you more than unto God, judge ye. For we cannot but speak the things which we have seen and heard.*
> (Acts 4:19-20)

Such was the courage of the Hebrew youths, who, unawed by the fiery furnace and unmoved by the example of a whole nation, disdained to comply with the royal edict and resolutely exposed themselves to a cruel death rather than violate the dictates of their conscience. (Daniel 3)

Thus, wherever the soul is clad with righteousness, it is emboldened both to do and suffer the will of God. Consequently, Satan's engine of persecution, whereby he has destroyed myriads, being divested of its power to intimidate the righteous, his dominion over them must for ever cease.

Lastly, righteousness will turn our weakness to strength. The powers of man, independent of divine grace, remain the same after conversion as before. Of himself he can do nothing. But, that divine principle which actuates the godly is mighty in operation. However, numerous or powerful their enemies may be, the 'grace of Christ is sufficient for them'. The weakest may say, 'through Christ strengthening me I can do all things'. Their inherent weakness does not at all militate against this assertion. For, when they are weakest in themselves, the Christian's strength is at its' height.

When they look unto their Lord for help,

...He will perfect His strength in their weakness.
(2 Corinthians 12:8-10)

Survey for a moment the Christian's conquests: His lusts are subdued, condemned, crucified. The world is overcome and put under his feet. The powers of darkness are put to flight and he is triumphing daily in the God of his salvation.

...strengthened is he with might in his inward man. That mighty are his weapons to destroy the strongholds of sin and Satan and to bring every thought into captivity to the obedience of Christ.
(Ephesians 3:16 & 2 Corinthians 10:5)

What shall we now say to you who are destitute of this armor? Shall we congratulate you on your prospects of victory? Shall we even flatter you with hopes of escaping with life? We cannot! We dare not! There is a possibility that you might vanquish an armed host with a broken pitcher or make the walls of an impregnable fortress to fall with the sound of ram's horns. But to succeed without righteousness in your spiritual warfare is impossible. For the truth of God is pledged. You shall perish if you continue in your unrighteous state.

... awake then to righteousness, and sin not.
(1 Corinthians 15:34)

Let your earnest prayer ascent up before God that you may be made new creatures in Christ Jesus, and be turned effectually from the power of Satan unto God. Do not mistake! Do not imagine that any righteousness which you can attain in your own strength will protect you, or that even that which is wrought in you by the Holy Spirit has in itself such mighty efficacy. That to which such glorious powers are ascribed is wrought in you by the Spirit of God. After all, it is not your inherent goodness, but the grace of God, that must preserve you from your enemies. Your implanted righteousness will indeed be made use of by Him. Still, God must be acknowledged as the sole author of all that is done either in or by you, and the glory must be given to Him alone.

To you who have:

...the armor of righteousness on the right hand and on the left.

(2 Corinthians 6:7)

We say:

...stand fast in the Lord.

(Philippians 3:1)

Let nothing prevail upon you to lay aside your breastplate for one moment. The instant you part with it you are shorn of your strength and are become weak as other men.

...hold fast then that ye have, that no man take your crown.

(Revelation 3:11)

Thus shall your subtle adversary be foiled in all his attacks. He shall never be able to inflict on you any deadly wound.

...then shall you not be ashamed when you have respect unto all God's commandments.

(Psalm 119:6)

90

As the righteousness of Christ sustained him amidst the fiercest assaults of his enemies, so shall you be preserved while fighting under His banners and following His commands. His express promise to you is,

> *...he that walketh uprightly, and worketh righteousness shall never be moved.*
>
> (Psalm 15:2)

And again,

> *...the Lord God is a sun and shield. He will give grace and glory. No good thing will be withheld from them that walk uprightly.*
>
> (Psalm 84:11)

CHAPTER SEVEN

The Christian's Greaves

Stand - having your feet shod with the preparation of the gospel of peace.

(Ephesians 6: 14, 15)

The third piece of armor Paul mentioned in Ephesians 6 has to do with the believer's feet.

...and your feet shod with the preparation of the gospel of peace.

(Ephesians 6:15)

This verse is usually interpreted to mean that the believer is to be prepared to preach the gospel of peace.

...how beautiful are the feet of them that preach the gospel of peace and bring glad tidings of good things.

(Romans 10:15)

is often cited as a parallel passage.

However, it is my opinion that Ephesians 6:15 refers to having the "message of peace' in our hearts rather than "preaching the message of peace." This is more in keeping with the context. In the spiritual warfare, Satan is out to destroy the peace in our hearts. He causes us to doubt and fret so that we are in turmoil of soul, thus part of the armor is to give us a settled walk that is peaceful.

> *...is our peace...*
>
> (Ephesians 2:14)

This passage tells us that Christ is our peace.

Many other scriptures speak of peace. The words of Jesus are recorded in:

> *...peace I leave with you, my peace I give unto you. Not as the world giveth, give I unto you. Let not your heart be troubled. Neither let it be afraid.*
>
> (John 14:27)

> *...these things I have spoken unto you that in me ye might have peace. In the world ye shall have tribulation. But, be of good cheer. I have over come the world.*
>
> (John 16:33)

Thus, we see that Christ is peace itself. When we possess Him we have true peace, for turmoil of soul disappears.

There are two kinds of peace spoken of in the New Testament: "Peace with God" and "Peace of God".

> *...therefore being justified by faith, we have peace with God through our Lord Jesus Christ.*
>
> (Romans 5:1)

This passage refers to "Peace with God". This kind of peace comes when we turn from our sin and receive Jesus

94

Christ as Savior. At that moment of decision we become children of God. Because Christ has paid the penalty for our sin, the moment we receive Him as Savior we are at peace with God. God tells us that he has,

> *...reconciled us to Himself by Jesus Christ.*
> (2 Corinthians 5:18)

Peace with God is also referred to in,

> *...the word which God sent unto the children of Israel, preaching peace by Jesus Christ.*
> (Acts 10:36)

Christ has thus secured our peace with God inasmuch as this peace is obtained by receiving Him as Savior. It is a permanent and settled relationship of peace with God that Satan's darts cannot disturb.

The scriptures also refer to the "Peace of God".

> *...be careful for nothing. But in every thing by prayer and supplication with thanksgiving let your requests be made known unto god. And the peace of God, which passeth all understanding, shall keep your hearts and minds through Jesus Christ.*
> (Philippians 4:6, 7)

Whereas, peace with God is a judicial peace in that we are made right with God by receiving Christ as Savior. The peace of God is an experiential peace. The life of believers is in great contrast to the life of unbelievers. Isaiah said,

> *...but the wicked are like the troubled sea, when it cannot rest, whose waters cast up mire and dirt. There is no peace, sayeth my God, to the wicked.*
> (Isaiah 57:20-21)

Since unbelievers are not at peace with God, it is not possible for them to experience the peace of God.

Consider the kind of peace God has. Nothing is able to upset or disturb Him. It is this kind of peace we can experience as we trust Him completely for everything.

Jesus wants His people to have this peace. On the Isle of Patmos, when John was given a revelation of Jesus Christ, John said,

> *...when I saw Him, I fell at His feet as dead. And He laid His right hand upon me, saying unto me, "fear not, I am the first and the last. I am He that liveth, and was dead. And, behold, I am alive for evermore, amen; and have the keys of hell and of death.*
>
> (Revelation 1:17-18)

Jesus also said of himself,

> *...I am Alpha and Omega, the beginning and the ending...which is, and which was, and which is to come, the Almighty.*
>
> (Revelation 1:8)

As we read these words concerning Christ we see His omnipotence and realize nothing or no one is able to defeat His program. He is allowing certain things to happen on earth now that go against His desires. Eventually Jesus Christ, Himself, will return to earth to establish His kingdom. He is not frustrated by the events that are now happening. Neither should the believer be frustrated by them, even though he is not able to understand them. If we could only see the future as God sees it, we would have no questions. But God has intended that we walk by faith instead of sight.

96

We will experience the peace of God as we realize the security we have in Him. Jesus said,

> ...*my sheep hear my voice, and I know them, and they follow me, and I give unto them eternal life. And they shall never perish, neither shall any man pluck them out of my hand. My father, which gave them me, is greater than all. And no man is able to pluck them out of my father's hand.*
>
> (John 10: 27-29)

So when Paul told believers that their feet should be "shod with the preparation of the gospel of peace", he was referring to the peace with God and the peace of God that is possible for everyone who knows Christ as their Savior. Christ died so that we could have peace with God and its' resulting peace of God, and through the Holy Spirit this peace is maintained in our hearts.

The question might be asked concerning Ephesians 6:15 : *"Why are the feet mentioned in connection with this peace?"* The significance lies in the fact that feet are symbolic of our daily walk, or life. The Lord Jesus Christ is presented here as God's provision of peace for daily living. In the process of daily living, there are many circumstances that give rise to fear. In fact, fear is one of the chief characteristics of the last days. Describing these last days, Jesus said,

> ...*men's hearts failing them for fear, and for look- ing after those things which are coming on the earth. For the powers of heaven shall be shaken.*
>
> (Luke 21:26)

The problems of fear and anxiety plague people the world over and much has been given to these subjects. However, the person who has peace through Jesus Christ

97

does not need to fear or to be anxious. Although we do not understand how events will turn out, we are to put all of our care on God, because he cares for us. (1 Peter 5:7)

The word in (Ephesians 6:15) translated "Preparation" means "Readiness". However, concerning this world, M.R. Vincent points out that "In Hellenistic Greek it was sometimes used in the sense of the establishment or firm foundation, which would suit this passage: Firm-Footing" (*word studies in the New Testament P. 867*) So with this solid footing of peace, we can publish the gospel of peace in a world of conflict and evil.

With this deep-seated peace, we can face the foe on every side with true confidence. The psalmist must have experienced this confidence for he wrote,

> *...it is vain for you to rise up early, to sit up late, to eat the bread of sorrows. For so He giveth His beloved sleep.*
>
> (Psalm 127:2)

> *...great peace have they which love Thy law. And nothing shall offend them.*
>
> (Psalm 119:165)

We need to learn to live a day at a time. We should claim for each day God's victory over tension and worry. We should commit the problems of the future to the Lord because only He knows what the future holds. Jesus spoke of the necessity of believers to have total reliance on Him each day. He said,

> *...take no thought for your life, what ye shall eat, or what ye shall drink. Nor yet for your body, what ye shall put on. Is not the life more than*

meat, and the body more than raiment?'
(Matthew 6:25)

Jesus did not mean that we were to make no plans for the future, but we are not to worry about the future over which we have no control.

Jesus further said,

> *...therefore, take no thought, saying, what shall we eat? Or, what shall we drink? Or, wherewithal shall we be clothed? (for after all these things do the gentiles seek) For your heavenly Father knoweth that ye have need of all these things. But seek ye first the Kingdom of God, and His righteousness; and all these things shall be added unto you. Take, therefore, no thought for the morrow. For the morrow shall take thought for the things of itself. Sufficient unto the day is the evil thereof.*

(Matthew 6:31-34)

To take "thought for the morrow" is to worry about the future, which Jesus says the believer should not do.

David saw the need of trusting the Lord for everything, thus he wrote,

> *...cast thy burden upon the Lord, and he shall sustain thee. He shall never suffer the righteous to be moved.*

(Psalm 55:22)

CHAPTER EIGHT

The Shield of Faith

Above all, taking the shield of faith, wherewith ye shall be able to quench all the fiery darts of the wicked.

Ephesians 6:16

The armor of the ancients was generally so constructed that it could repel any weapon that might come against it. Yet the warrior did not conceive himself to be completely armed without a shield. In reference to the Christian soldier, this observation may be applied with still greater propriety because, however excellent the different pieces of his armor may be, not one of them will suffice for his protection unless it is itself also covered by the shield of faith. As,

...without faith it is impossible to please God.

(Hebrews 11:6)

So, without faith it is impossible to withstand Satan; that powerful adversary will soon pierce through our "truth'

101

and "righteousness' if they be exposed to his assault without any additional defense. On this account the apostle directs, that "above all" and in addition to all, we should "take the shield of faith".

The wicked is literally 'the wicked one' and refers to Satan. Notice the two "alls" in this verse: "Above all" and "All the fiery darts".

Two Points

1. The office of faith in the Christian's armor

2. Its' transcendent excellence

The particular use of a shield is to ward off a blow from any part of the body that may be menaced and for the end it is to be applied in every direction as occasion may require.

Now Satan strikes sometimes at one part and sometimes at another according as the different parts may seem most open to his attack. The temptations with which he makes his assaults are as 'fiery darts which fly with incredible velocity and are calculated to inflame the soul with their deadly poison.

The office of faith, and its' power to repel these darts, will distinctly appear while we show how it enables the Christian to foil Satan in all his attempts to wound either his head or heart.

The shield of faith refers to the Lord Jesus Christ who is God's provision for our protection. It is through faith in Jesus Christ that we are completely protected against the attacks of Satan. The basis of our overcoming in the spiritual warfare is our faith in Christ.

The Bible says:

> *...for whatsoever is born of God overcometh the world. And this is the victory that overcometh the world, even our faith. Who is he that overcometh the world, but he that believeth that Jesus is the Son of God?*

(1 John 5:4-5)

We are the overcomers because of our faith in Jesus Christ who is,

> *...the author and finisher of our faith.*

(Hebrews 12:2)

Satan has many fierce and fiery temptations whereby he endeavors to wound the head. There is not anything so horrid or blasphemous which he will not suggest to the mind. Even atheism is not so shocking, but he is capable of impressing the idea of it upon the soul, and of leading men to an adoption of it in practice, at least, if not also in theory and judgment.

He will take occasion also from the difficulties that there are in scripture to draw men to infidelity. He suggests: How can that be the word of God which is so full of contradictions? And who can know with any certainty what it declares to us when those who profess to believe it are of such opposite sentiments?

But there are other temptations whereby Satan labors to turn from the faith those who confess the divine authority of the scriptures. He will draw them into "errors" of various kinds, and thus undermine the principles which he could not destroy by open assault.

Mark the different heresies and examine them by this test, and the truth of the observation will immediately appear. Because our Savior was man, and both lived and died as an example to His followers, therefore the Socinians (Unitarians) affirm that he was only man. And, that He died only as an example. Thus they set aside both His deity and atonement. Because the Spirit of God is represented as dwelling in believers, therefore, the mystics reduce all religion to a vain conceit about the "light" within them. They approach Christianity from a regard to which they overlook the work of Christ for them, and supersede the plainest institutions of religion. In a very great degree, they overlook the scriptures themselves.

To enter more minutely into these various heresies would lead us too far from our subject. The point to be illustrated is, how does faith enable us to avoid them?

Previous to this inquiry, it will be proper to show briefly that these errors do indeed proceed from Satan as their author, and that they are not unfairly compared to fiery darts.

Nothing could be plainer in the scriptures than that Satan is the great author of error. Not only because he is ..."*the father of lies*", and "*the deceiver of the world*" (John 8:44 & Revelation 12:9).

But because the propagators of error are expressly called his children, and his ministers, and they who have embraced error are said to have been "...*tempted of the tempter*" and to have "*turned aside after Satan*" and to be 'of the synagogue of Satan' (1 Thessalonians 3:5; 1 Timothy 5:15; Revelation 2:9).

This point will receive additional confirmation by observing with what propriety his temptations are compared to "fiery darts", for how suddenly they strike the mind! How deeply also do they penetrate! And with what venom do they inflame the soul! Truly,

> *...they set on fire the whole course of nature, and themselves are set on fire of hell.*

(James 3:6)

Paul speaks of those who are turned from the truth as being "*...bewitched*" (Galatians 3:1).

And indeed, when we see what infatuation seizes them, how their understandings are blinded, their judgments warped, their conscience perverted, and how they are carried away by their own pride and self-sufficiency, without ever considering what spirit they are of, or conceiving it possible that they should be misled, we cannot, but confess that they are the unhappy victims of Satanic agency.

Now we come to the point proposed. "To consider how faith repels these fiery darts".

Faith, provided it is a true and living faith, receives the Word of God simply on the authority of Him that revealed it. It staggers not at any difficulties either in the dispensations of His providence or the declarations of His grace. Conscious of man's inability to comprehend even the most common matters in their full extent, the believer submits his reason to God, and receives without gainsaying whatsoever divine wisdom has revealed. Now the sovereignty of God in the government of the world, even in the falling of a sparrow, or in the hairs of our head, is most clearly asserted in the inspired volume. And, on that account, no occurrence whatever is suffered to weaken the conviction that all things are under His immediate control. Nor do the difficulties that are in scripture at all lessen its' authority in the believer's eyes. Whatever he cannot account for as arising from the circumstances under which the scriptures have been handed down to us, he puts to the score of his own ignorance and contentedly says, "What I know not now, I shall know hereafter". And, as to all the heresies that have been broached in the Christian church he has one way of repelling all. He *"...compares spiritual things with spiritual"* (1 Corinthians 2:13) not hastily rejecting any plain declaration of God because he cannot discern its' harmony and agreement with some other declaration. He rather looks to God for the teachings of His Spirit, and keeps his mind ready to embrace whatever may lead to his own humiliation or to the glory of God. If it be thought, that in this way he will be as open to receive error as truth, we answer, that God has promised to *"...guide him into all truth."* (John 16:13)

Every believer has within himself the witness of all the fundamental doctrines of our religion. So that, through he be a mere fool in all other matters, he shall surely be kept from error in the concerns of his soul.

We must next call your attention to the temptations wherewith Satan assaults the heart. Under this term we include both the will and the affections. The will he endeavors to weaken by terrors, while he corrupts the affections by the allurement of sense.

As soon as that wicked fiend beholds any turning unto God, he will suggest to their minds the comforts they must sacrifice, the reproaches they must incur, the losses they must sustain, and the insuperable difficulties they must encounter, that so he may shake their resolution and divert them from their purpose. It was thus that for a time he prevented the entrance of the Israelites into Canaan. It was thus also that he succeeded in dampening the ardor of that wealthy youth, who, from love of his great possessions, relinquished all hope of an interest in Christ. In the same manner does he prevail with thousands of the present day who would gladly participate in gospel blessings if they could retain together with them their carnal attachments.

If Satan cannot succeed by these means, he will represent their case as hopeless. Thus through hopelessness he dissuades them from prosecuting their course by the consideration that their efforts will be in vain.

To others Satan will propose the pleasures of sins. He will set before them, as he did before our Lord, the glory of the world. He will draw their attention to "the lust of the eye and the pride of life". He will represent these things in the most fascinating view, well knowing that if he can but induce them to love the pleasures, the riches, or the honors of the world, he has accomplished his purpose and effectually alienated their hearts from God.

Now these also are as 'fiery darts' which, if they once enter into the soul, will burn up all the good that is within it, and destroy it utterly.

But faith is as useful to protect the heart as to defend the head. As it obviates every difficulty that may perplex the understanding, so it wards off everything that may intimidate or defile the soul.

To the temptations that assault the will, faith opposes the importance of eternal things. Be it so; I must endure much if I will adhere to my purpose of serving God. But, what shall I have to endure if I do not serve Him?" It is not a matter of mere choice, but of absolute necessity. For, "what shall it profit me if I gain the whole world and lose my own soul?" Let me not then hear of difficulties. For if Nebuchadnezzar's furnace was before me, I know it would be better to suffer martyrdom at once with the Hebrew youths than to renounce my allegiance to God. With respect to the hopelessness of my case, nothing but destruction can result from despair. For to whom can I go if not to Him who has the words of eternal life? God helping me, therefore, I will go forward. And, if I perish, I will perish at the foot of my Redeemer's cross, crying for mercy as the chief of sinners.

Then to the temptations that assault the affections, faith opposes the excellency of eternal things. Moses may have argued, "True, I might enjoy the pleasures of sin, but would they equal the pleasure of serving God, and especially those "pleasures which are at His right hand for evermore?" Are not "the unsearchable riches in Christ, together with the honor that cometh of God, sufficient to counterbalance all riches or honors that I may forego for Christ's sake? Avaunt Satan! For what you offer me is poor, transient, and delusive. The blessedness of the saints, both in this world and the next, is "substantial, exquisite, and everlasting."

...when he was come to years, refused to be called the son of Pharaoh's daughter; choosing rather to suffer affliction with the people of God, than to enjoy the pleasures of sin for a season; esteeming

108

the reproach of Christ greater riches than the treasures in Egypt.

(Hebrews 11:24-26)

The principle that dictated the argument was "faith". This was his shield. And the same will enable us also to repel the darts of Satan, however fiercely they be hurled and however formidably they may come against us.

Having thus illustrated the office of faith, we proceed to point out, its transcendent excellence.

Somewhat of this has already appeared. But, the high encomium which the apostle bestows on this piece of armor in particular above all others manifestly demands a more distinct consideration.

We may observe then in commendation of faith considered as the Christian's shield, that its use is universal. Its application is easy. Its success is sure.

First, its use is universal. All the other parts of armor have their distinct province, to which they are confined. "Truth" and "Righteousness" defend the heart, but they are of no use at all to protect the head. But "Faith" is universally applicable to every species of temptation. Faith discerns the truth of the gospel, and thereby is fitted to preserve the head from error. It discerns also the importance and excellence of the gospel, and is therefore proper to preserve the heart from sin. It is no less useful to the feet, for we "...*stand by faith*", and "*walk by faith*". (2 Corinthians 1: 24; 5:7)

Every step we take is safest under the guidance of faith, because it both affords us the best light and enables us to walk without stumbling even in the dark.

109

Let this consideration then operate on all and stir us all up to seek faith. Let us not hastily conclude that we possess this principle, for *"...all men have not faith"*. (2 Thessalonians 3:2), *"...faith is a gift of God."*

Nor can we have it unless it has been given us from above. We should all seek it at the hands of a reconciled God. Don't be satisfied with "the girdle of sincerity" or the "breastplate of righteousness" or the "greaves of the gospel of peace". They are all good and useful in their place. But, it is faith that gives even to them their chief strength. And, it is faith by which alone you can ever be victorious. Does the world tempt you?

> *...this is the victory that overcometh the world, even your faith.*
>
> (1 John 5:4)

Does corruption harass you? You must *"...purify your heart by faith."* (Acts 15:9)

Do your graces languish? It is faith alone that will set them to work in a way of love. And lastly, does the devil, as a roaring lion threaten to devour you? It is by being steadfast in the faith that you must resist and vanquish him. Think then of the use and efficacy of faith; and pray to our adorable Savior in the words of His apostles, *"...Lord, increase our faith"* (Luke 17:5).

In the next place we observe that its application is easy. A shield is easily transferred from one position to another as occasion may require. Faith also quickly moves to the protection of any part that is attacked. We do not say that it is an easy thing to produce faith, for it requires no less power than that which was exerted in raising Christ from the dead to create faith in the heart. But when a person has faith, then we say it is easy for him to apply it for his defense. Suppose that our head were attacked with his subtle heresies, and we had nothing but reason to counteract the temptation. How weak, how tardy, how uncertain would be its' operation! The greater part of mankind would not have either time or ability to follow Satan in all his arguments, nor would those of the strongest intellect ever arrive at certainty. They could rise no higher than opinion at the least, while those of inferior talents would be lost in endless perplexity.

Suppose again that our heart were attacked with some fiery lust and we had no better defense than that which reason could afford. Would passion listen to the voice of reason? As well might we attempt to extinguish flames that were consuming our house by a slight sprinkling or water with the hand as to stop the course of our passions by the efforts of unassisted reason. But, in either of these cases one single word from scripture will suffice. How was it that our Great Captain repelled the fiery darts that were cast at Him?

...it is written, it is written again, it is written.
(Matthew 4:1-11)

Thus He fought and His vanquished enemy fled from before Him. Thus also must we fight. By opposing to our enemy this shield, the weakest and most ignorant is as sure of victory as the strongest and most intelligent. In some respects the poor and ignorant have an advantage over the rich and learned because they exercise faith, for the most part, in a simpler manner. Whereas, the others are ever trusting, more or less, to their own reason and it is expressly with a view to confound the pride of reason that God has given this superiority to the poor, and has *"...chosen them"* (James 2:5) in preference to others, to be rich in faith.

Let this then operate as a further inducement with us to seek faith, since none of us can get the victory without it and, by it the very weakest on earth shall be able to remove mountains.

Lastly, we may affirm, that its success is sure. But for their faith the most eminent of God's saints would have been destroyed *"...I had fainted, if I had not believed"* (Psalm 27:13) said David. Peter would have been driven away as the chaff if our Lord had not secured his faith from failing. On the other hand, we have a host of saints upon record, who,

> *...through faith subdued kingdoms, wrought righteousness, obtained promises, stopped the mouths of lions, quenched the violence of fire, escaped the edge of the sword, out of weakness were made strong, waxed valiant in fight, turned to flight the armies of the aliens. Women received their dead raised to life again, and others obtain a better resurrection. And others had trials of cruel mockings and scourgings, yes of bonds and imprisonment. They were stoned, they were sawn asunder, were tempted, and were slain with the sword. They wandered about in sheep-skins and goat-skins, being destitute, afflicted, tormented. These all obtained a good report through faith.*
> (Hebrews 11:33-39)

Further, if we search the annals of the world, we shall not find one single instance wherein believers were ultimately vanquished. On many occasions they have been wounded, and sorely too. Even the Father of the faithful, Himself, was not so expert in the use of His shield as to ward off every blow. But believers are secured from any fatal stroke. Our Lord has pledged His word:

> ...*that they shall never perish. That if they fall they shall be raised up again to renew the contest and that Satan shall finally be bruised under their feet.*
> (John 10:28; Micah 7:8; Romans 16:20)

Remarkable in this view are the expressions of the text. The idea of quenching the fiery darts of the wicked one may perhaps refer to the custom of making shields sometimes of raw hides, that in case a poisoned arrow should perforate them, the wound, which on account of the poison must otherwise have been fatal, might be healed. But, perhaps the true meaning may be, that by faith we shall as completely defeat the malignant efforts of Satan as by the extinguishing of fire we shall be delivered from its' fury. This is not true for just some temptations only. It extends to "all" without exception. Nor can it be said of some believers only, who are of the highest class. For all who are armed with the shield of faith, whether they be old or young, rich or poor, learned or unlearned, "shall be able" perfectly, and forever, to subdue their adversary.

To all then we say,

> ...*have faith in God. If ye have believed in the Father, believe also in Christ. Believe in the Lord, so shall ye be established. Believe His prophets, so shall ye prosper.*
> (Mark 11:22; John 14:1; 2 Chronicles 20:20)

CHAPTER NINE

The Christian Helmet

And take the Helmet of Salvation...

The generality of mankind have very inadequate ideas of the Christian warfare. They know but little of the enemies which whom we have to contend, or of the imminent danger to which we are exposed through their continual assaults. As some conception might be formed of the power of an enemy by viewing the extensive preparations that were made to oppose them, so may we learn to estimate the difficulties of the spiritual warfare by surveying the various parts of armor which God has prepared for our defense. We have already noticed the girdle and breastplate for the body, the greaves for the legs and feet, the shield for the head, in common with the rest of the body. Yet the head is not sufficiently protected. It must have a piece of armor more appropriate – a piece suited to its necessities and fitted for its' use. In the account given us of Goliath, we read:

...he had an helmet of brass upon his head.
(1 Samuel 17:5)

Such a piece of armor is provided for us also. We are required to 'take the helmet of salvation'

Opening this subject we shall show:

1. What are we to understand by "salvation"

2   The use and importance of salvation in the Christian warfare

WHAT ARE WE TO UNDERSTAND BY THE TERM "SALVATION"?

It is evident that the expression is elliptical (or incomplete); nor would we know how, with any certainty, to complete the sense if the apostle himself had not supplied the defect in a parallel passage. All doubt is removed by that exhortation in his epistle to the Thessalonians.

...let us who are of the day, be sober, putting on the breastplate of faith and love, and for an helmet, the hope of salvation.
(1 Thessalonians 5:8)

From this we see that hope is the Christian's helmet. Yet, because there are various kinds of hope, and only one that will afford the Christian any effectual protection, we must enter more particularly into the subject and distinguish the scriptural hope from every other that may be mistaken for it.

In the first place then, true hope has salvation for its object. This is very strongly marked in different parts of

116

scripture. For we are said to *"...be saved by hope"* (Romans 8:24) and salvation itself is sometimes called hope. They who look for salvation are said to be looking for that blessed hope. (Titus 2:13) At other times hope is called salvation. We are exhorted in the text to take the helmet of salvation. There are many whose hopes have respect indeed to eternal life, but they are unmindful of their lost estate. They are regardless of that way of deliverance which God has provided for them through the blood and righteousness of the Lord Jesus. If they have sinned, they have not sinned in such a degree as to deserve the wrath of God. They have committed only common and venial faults. They have, moreover, done many things to counterbalance their evil deeds, and therefore they hope for heaven as the award of justice rather than as a gift of unbounded mercy. This, for distinction sake, we may call a self-righteous hope. The hope of every true Christian is founded altogether on the merits of Christ and has respect to salvation as purchased for us by His obedience and death.

Further, true hope has God for its' author. There is scarcely a person to be found in the world, who, if the question were put to him, "do you hope to go to heaven in your present state", would not answer in the affirmative. If we should proceed to enquire, "Where did you get that hope?" they would tell us that they had always had it. But this is a presumptuous hope; the offspring of ignorance and conceit. Widely different from this is the Christian's hope.

> *...he had trembled for his state. He has seen his guilt and danger. He had fled for refuge to the hope set before him.*

> (Hebrews 6:18)

God has revealed to him the riches of His grace, and has shown him that,

> ...*where sin abounded, grace did much more abound.*
>
> (Romans 5:20)

The Holy Spirit has,

> ...*taken of the things of Christ, and shown them unto him.*
>
> (John 16:14; 1 John 1:7; Acts 13:39)

He has convinced him that,

> ...*the blood of Jesus Christ is able to cleanse him from all sin...*
>
> (John 16:14; 1 John 1:7; Acts 13:39)

and that,

> ...*all who believe in Christ are justified from all things.*
>
> (John 16:14; 1 John 1:7; Acts 13:39)

In this way God has inspired him with hope, that, notwithstanding all his past iniquities, he shall obtain salvation; and though there may be a considerable difference as to the degree of fear or terror that may precede this hope, yet this is the way in which it is invariably wrought in the soul. Hence it is said,

> "...*God begets unto a lively hope*" and "*gives us everlasting consolation and good hope through grace*" and that "*he fills us with joy and peace in believing, that we may abound in hope through the power of the Holy Ghost.*" (1 Peter 1:3; 2 Thessalonians 2:16; Romans 15:13)

Once more: True hope has holiness for its' inseparable

companion. Whatever may be imagined to the contrary, there is no salvation to those who live in sin. Christ came to "*...save us from our sins*" (Matthew 1:21).

Not in them. We are expressly told that

> ...*the grace of God, which bringeth salvation, teaches us, that denying ungodliness and worldly lusts, we should live righteously, soberly, and godly in this present world, looking for that blessed hope, and the glorious appearing of the great God and our Savior, Jesus Christ.*
>
> (Titus 2:11-13)

There is a kind of hope that will consist with the indulgence of secret lust, and with a total want of holy dispositions. But, that is "*...the hope of the hypocrite, which perisheth*" (Job 8:13) and shall be swept away with the besom of Job. But the hope of the upright is far different from this. It will admit of no allowed sin; whether of omission or of commission. On the contrary, we are told that,

> ...*he who hath this hope in him purifieth himself even as God is pure.*
>
> (1 John 3:3)

He will retain no bosom lusts. He will not as much as wish for any exceptions and reserves in his obedience to God. He will desire and endeavor to be,

> ...*holy as God is holy, and perfect even as his Father that is in heaven is perfect.*
>
> (1 Peter 1:16; Matthew 5:48)

This then may serve to distinguish the Christian's hope from that which is self-righteous, presumptuous, or hypocritical; and consequently, to determine with considerable accuracy what that hope is that is connected with salvation.

Though the text itself does not so much as mention hope, and much less discriminate between its' different kinds, yet the very omission of these things points out the evident propriety of marking clearly what the import of salvation is, and what that is which alone deserves the name.

We may now, with much greater advantage, proceed to show,

THE USE AND IMPORTANCE OF SALVATION IN THE CHRISTIAN WARFARE

The importance of this helmet is not obscurely intimated in that prophecy respecting Christ, wherein it is said,

> *...he put on righteousness as a breastplate, and an helmet of salvation upon His head.*
> (Isaiah 59:17)

But, to mark it more distinctly, we may observe, that it prepares us for conflicts, sustains us in them, and brings us victorious through them.

Hope prepares us for conflicts. A man armed with a helmet feels himself ready to battle. He fears not to meet his adversary, because he had a defense which, he trusts, will prove sufficient for his preservation. Thus a man that has a hope of salvation enters into the combat with holy confidence. He is not intimidated by the frowns of an ungodly world, because he,

> *...knows in whom he has believed and that God is able to keep that which He has committed to Him.*
> (2 Timothy 1:12)

He says with David,

> *...though an host should encamp against me, my heart shall not fear. Though war should rise against me, in this will I be confident.*
>
> (Psalm 27: 3)

This subject cannot be more strongly illustrated than in Caleb and the whole nation of the Israelites. The nation was terrified at the report of the spies, and, instead of proceeding to fight against the Canaanites, proposed to appoint a captain, and go back into Egypt. But, Caleb, whose hope was lively, stood unmoved and strove to animate his country men with an assurance of easy victory. Thus, while the hearts of others were failing them for fear, and they would *"...turn back into perdition"* (1 Samuel 30:6) the true Christian *"...encourages himself in his God"* and makes up his mind to die or conquer.

Further, a true hope will sustain us in conflicts. Many who have shown intrepidity at first have yet fainted when their trials were severe and of long continuance. He who has a hope full of immortality will never yield, however painful the conflict may be and however heavy the pressure. The patriarch's continued to sojourn in the land of promise as mere pilgrims notwithstanding they had frequent opportunity to return to their own country and kindred. But, they accounted the trail as nothing because,

> *...they looked for a better country, that is, an heavenly.*
>
> (Hebrews 11:10, 14-16)

Many women also who were tortured by the most ingenious cruelty even unto death, yet declined accepting deliverance upon dishonorable terms, that they might be counted worthy to obtain a better resurrection. Paul too, that bright pattern of all virtues, assigns this as the reason why he did not faint under his unparalleled afflictions.

> *...His outward man decayed, but his inward man was renewed day by day; and his afflictions appeared to him light and momentary because he looked from the vanities of time and sense to the invisible realities of eternity.*
>
> (2 Corinthians 4:16-18)

Thus shall our trials rather confirm than weaken our hope, provided it be scriptural and genuine.

> *...our tribulation shall work patience; our patience, experience; and our experience, hope.*
>
> (Romans 5:3-4)

Once more: True faith will bring us victorious through our conflicts. The Lord Jesus Christ, himself, in this respect fully verified the prophecies respecting Him, and set us an example which it is our privilege to follow. The prophet Isaiah represents Jesus as speaking in these triumphant strains.

> *...the Lord God will help me. Therefore shall I not be confounded. Therefore have I set my face like a flint and I know that I shall not be ashamed. He is near that justifieth me. Who will contend with me? Let us stand together. Who is mine adversary? Let him come near to me. Behold, the Lord God will help me. Who is he that shall condemn me? Lo, they all shall wax old as a garment. The moth shall eat them up.*
>
> (Isaiah 50:7-9)

Thus will hope enable us also to anticipate the victory while yet we are fighting on the field of battle. Through it we may defy all the powers of earth or hell ever to,

> ...*separate us from the love of God that is in Christ Jesus.*
>
> (Romans 8:39)

Yes, such an anchor shall it be to our souls, that we shall be steadfast in the midst of this tempestuous world, and be enabled to outride the storm which causes many to "...*make shipwreck of their faith*" (1 Timothy 1:19) and ultimately sinks them to everlasting perdition.

Let me entreat you, first, to get this helmet. Do not be satisfied with a delusive hope that will fail you in the day of necessity, but bring it to the trial. See whether it is able to endure the assaults of your adversary. Compare it with the description which God himself gives of that which is true and saving. Look well to it that it is not self-righteous, presumptuous, or hypocritical. Be well assured that it is of heavenly temper, and let daily experience show that it enables you to 'lift up your head above all your enemies' whether outward or inward, terrestrial or infernal. Think with yourselves how awful it would be to find, either in the hour of death or in the day of judgment, that you had deceived yourselves with some phantom of your own imagination, and formed expectations of happiness that cannot be realized. Do not expose yourselves to such a dreadful disappointment. Remember the fate of the foolish virgins. They hoped that their lamp of profession would suffice though they were destitute of the oil whereby alone they could make their light to shine. Through this they perished, as thousands of others have done, by resting in their religious privileges, or their outward conformity to the divine will, when they had not the inward principle of renewing, sanctifying grace. But let it not be so with you.

>...*hope that shall never make you ashamed.*
>
> (1 Corinthians 11:31; Romans 5:5)

Next, we would urge you to keep on this helmet in all our conflicts. Constant will be Satan's endeavors to deprive you of it; and great his triumph if he succeeds. Above all things be careful that you,

>...*cast not away your confidence, but hold fast the rejoicing of your hope, firm unto the end.*
>
> (Hebrews 10:35, 3:6)

If at any time you begin to be distracted with doubts and fear, instantly check yourselves as David did.

>...*Why art thou cast down, o my soul; and why art thou disquieted within me? Hope thou in God.*
>
> (Psalm 42:11)

Though you are to,

>...*work out your own salvation with fear and trembling...not run as uncertainly, or fight as one that beateth the air.*

You must remember who is engaged for your support, and that *"...he is faithful who hath promised."* (Hebrews 10:23)

It is true,

>...*you have need of patience, that after you have done the will of God you may receive the promise...*(but)...*if you hope for that you see not (such a*

124

hope implies that) you will with patience wait for it.

(Hebrews 10:36; Romans 8:25)

James proposes to you the example of the husbandman,

...behold, the husbandman waiteth for the precious fruit of the earth, and hath long patience for it until he receive the early and latter rain. Be ye also patient. Establish your hearts for the coming of the Lord draweth nigh; and then shall your confidence be richly rewarded.

(James 5:7-8)

...gird up then the loins of your mind. Be sober, and hope to the end for the grace that shall be brought unto you at the revelation of Jesus Christ.

(1 Peter 1:13)

This is the way, the sure way, to conquer.

...be steadfast, unmovable, always abounding in the work of the Lord. Knowing assuredly that your labor shall not be in vain in the Lord.

(1 Corinthians 15:58)

Lastly, let that which is your defense be also your ornament. There is not a more ornamental part of the soldier's armor than the helmet. Nor is there anything that more adorns the Christian than a lively, steadfast, and consistent hope. In the exercise of hope he stands, as it were, on the top of Pisgah and surveys the land of promise, the land that floweth with milk and honey. He longs to leave this dreary wilderness, and to *"...enter into the joy of his Lord"* (Matthew 25:21, 23) knowing that,

...when his earthly tabernacle shall be dissolved, he has a house not made with hands eternal in

125

*the heavens, he groans, earnestly desiring that
mortality may be swallowed up of life.*
(2 Corinthians 5:1-4)

If he had crowns and kingdoms in his possession, still he
would account it "...*far better to depart and to be with
Christ.*" (Philippians 1:23)

He is "...*looking for hasting to the coming of the day of
Christ,*" (2 Peter 3:12) and thus has 'his conversation in
heaven', while he remains a sojourner upon earth. View
the Christian in this frame, and confess that the sun shin-
ing in his meridian strength glorious as it is, has no glory,
by reason of the Christian's "glory that excelleth."

This, Christians, is the state in which you ought to live.
Were you more habitually in this frame, your years of warfare would seem as nothing, for the greatness of the prize
for which you contend. You can scarcely conceive what
energy such a frame would give to your souls. You would
soon come to Jesus with joy and wonder, like His disciples
of old, saying:

*...I beheld Satan as lightning fall from heaven.
Behold, I give unto you power to tread on serpents
and scorpions, and over all the power of the
enemy, and nothing shall by any means hurt you.*
(Luke 10:17-19)

Do but consider how weak will Satan's temptations be
when you thus abound in hope! How little will any thing be
able to move you when you are thus, by joyful anticipation,
already,

...sitting with Christ in heavenly places.
(Ephesians 2:6)

126

This is your perfection,

> *...you will come behind in no gift when you are thus waiting for the coming of the Lord Jesus.*
>
> (1 Corinthians 1:7)

Whatever you have to do, you will do it heartily, as unto the Lord, and not unto men,

> *...knowing that ye shall receive the reward of the inheritance.*
>
> (Colossians 3:24)

May God enable you thus to live, until faith shall be lost in sight and hope be consummated in enjoyment!

CHAPTER TEN

Sword of the Spirit

Take...the sword of the Spirit, which is the Word of God...

Ephesians 6:17

The sixth and final part of the armor to be taken by the believer is "the sword of the spirit, which is the Word of God.' The sword of the spirit is not an instrument to be placed in the believer's hand. It, too, refers to the protection given by the Lord Jesus Christ, even as the other pieces or the armor refer to an aspect of Christ's protection. Notice what the sword of the spirit is – "The Word of God". The gospel of John refers to Jesus Christ as the "Word," especially in John 1:1-14 this gospel begins:

In the beginning was the Word, and the Word was with God, and the Word was God.

(v.1)

This passage concludes with:

...and the Word was made flesh, and dwelt among us, and we beheld His glory, the glory as of the only begotten of the Father, full or grace and truth.

(v. 14)

These verses reveal that the "Word" refers specifically to the Lord Jesus Christ who left heaven's glory to take upon himself the form of a man and die on the cross for the sins of the world.

The Bible is also referred to as God's Word (note several verses in Psalm 119). As has been indicated previously, the difference is that Jesus Christ is the Living Word and the Bible is the Written Word. The two are brought together in,

...God who at sundry times and in divers manners spake in time past unto the fathers by the prophets, hath in these last days spoken unto us by His Son, whom He hath appointed heir of all things, by whom also He made the worlds.

(Hebrews 1:1-2)

God gave the written word through the prophets, and he gave the Living Word when He gave His only Son to come to earth.

Jesus told of the necessity of assimilating the Living and Written Word, and his comments are recorded in the gospel of John.

...Jesus said, I am the Living Bread which came down from Heaven. If any man eat of this bread, he shall live for ever; and the bread that I will

130

give is my flesh, which I will give for the life of the world.

(John 6:51)

The Jews could not understand how Jesus could give them His flesh to eat. Jesus added,

> *...whoso eateth my flesh, and drinketh my blood, hath eternal life; and I will raise him up at the last day. For my flesh is meat indeed, and my blood is drink indeed. He that eateth my flesh, and drinketh my blood, dwelleth in me, and I in him. As the Living Father hath sent me, and I live by the Father; so he that eateth me, even he shall live by me.*

(John 6:53-57)

Many turned back from following Jesus because of these words which they could not understand. But Jesus gave the clue to their meaning,

> *...it is the spirit that quickeneth (makes alive). The flesh profiteth nothing. The words that I speak unto you, they are spirit, and they are life.*

(John 6:63)

Jesus did not intend for his flesh to be literally eaten. He was emphasizing the need for his message to be completely assimilated and obeyed. It was the same as if he would have told his followers that they needed to feed upon Him and His word.

The word is referred to as "*...milk*" (1 Peter 2:2), and "*...meat*" (Hebrews 5:14).

Thus, the word is spiritual food for the believer. Jeremiah said,

...thy words were found, and I did eat them, and the word was unto me the joy and rejoicing of mine heart. For I am called by thy name, O Lord God of Hosts.

(Jeremiah 15:16)

By this statement, Jeremiah was saying that he fed upon the message contained in the Word of God. The psalmist said,

...how sweet are thy words unto my taste! Yea, sweeter than honey to my mouth!

(Psalm 119:103)

God's "written word" came to us by inspiration.

...all scripture is given by inspiration of God.
(2 Timothy 3:16)

The "Living Word" came to us by incarnation.

...The Word was made flesh, and dwelt among us.

(John 1:14)

The Written Word (Bible) and the Living Word (Christ) are inseparable. The Written Word is the message of the Living Word. Those who love the Living Word also love the Written Word for it tells about Him. To be careless about our relationship with the Written Word is also to be careless about our relationship with the Living Word.

It is the ministry of the Holy Spirit to reveal Christ to the believer (John 16:15).

He does this by revealing to the believer the truths of the Written Word. This is why the Bible is referred to as the "Sword of the Spirit". It is the method by which the Spirit works in our lives, making Christ real to us.

> *...for the word of God is quick (living) and powerful, and sharper than any two-edged sword, piercing even to the dividing asunder of soul and spirit, and of the joints and marrow, and is a discerner of the thoughts and intents of the heart.*
>
> (Hebrews. 4:12)

The power of His spoken word is seen in (Genesis 1) for God spoke and the result was creation.

As part of the believer's armor, the Word of God is to be used primarily as a defense against Satan's attacks. Christ himself gave us and example of how to meet the attacks of Satan by the Written Word. (Matthew 4:1-11).

The degree to which we will be able to use the Sword of the Spirit depends on the degree to which we allow it to penetrate our hearts. That is, to become real and living within us. This involves more than just memorizing the scriptures by putting the message of the Word of God into action in our lives. It is not what they say. Even Satan knows what the scriptures say, but he rejects the message, and even comes as an angel of light quoting it to deceive others. Just as Satan did with Eve, he can raise questions about something God has said and in that way plant doubts in a person's mind. There is no substitute for our knowing what the scriptures teach and for doing what it requires. As we have seen concerning the believer's armor, it is particularly important that we know what the scriptures say about our relationship to God.

Not only is the Sword of the Spirit, the Bible, to be used defensively against the attacks of Satan, but we are also to use it offensively in seeking to win others to Christ. Jesus commanded:

...go ye into all the world and preach the gospel to every creature.

(Mark 16:15)

We should always use the scriptures when helping someone see his need of Christ. The Bible is the only authoritative Word of God so it is the basis we must use in telling others of their sin and their need to receive Christ as Savior. Because the Bible is the only authoritative revelation from God, Paul urged Timothy,

...preach the Word; be instant in season, out of season; reprove, rebuke, exhort with all longsuffering and doctrine.

(2 Timothy 4:2)

To be able to use the Sword of the Spirit effectively, either defensively or offensively, calls for the greatest degree of spiritual devotion to Christ. Mere repetition of words does not make an efficient sword. But when the sword of the spirit is spoken from a heart that is filled with the spirit, there will be eternal benefits.

The sword must be ready at a moment's notice because Satan attacks without warning. He does not wait until we have our Bibles open and are reading God's word before he attacks. He often waits for the opposite – when our minds are farthest from the Word. However, even though we may not have the Bible available to read at the moment it can be available if we have memorized portions of it. In times of need, the spirit will bring to our attention the truths of God's Word if we have spent time thinking deeply on them in the past. It is one of the Holy Spirit's ministries to bring things to our memory.

> *...but the Comforter, which is the Holy Ghost, whom the Father will send in my name, He shall teach you all things, and bring all things to your remembrance whatsoever I have said unto you.*
>
> (John 14:26)

In this way, the Word becomes a sword of the spirit even though we may not have the Bible available to read. So it is important that we hide the word in our hearts, even as David did. (Psalm 119:11)

It is well to remember that, in witnessing, our responsibility is to set forth the Word. We do not need to defend it. On commenting about the lack of need to defend the Word, Spurgeon pointed out that one does not need to defend the Word any more than he needs to defend a lion. Let the lion out of his cage and he will defend himself.

CHAPTER ELEVEN

Resources for Victory

EPHESIANS 6:18-20

In the Book of Ephesians, prayer reaches the highest pinnacle of any place in the Bible. Two of Paul's prayers are recorded in this book. The first prayer (Ephesians 1:15-21) was for the believers to have the *"Spirit of Wisdom and Revelation"* in the knowledge of Christ. The second prayer (Ephesians 3:14-21) was for believers to have an *"Experiential"* knowledge of Christ's indwelling work within believers.

In connection with the spiritual armor of believers, another reference is made to prayer.

> *...Praying always with all prayer and supplication in the spirit, and watching thereunto with all perseverance and supplication for all saints.*
> (Ephesians 6:18)

Here we see that in addition to taking on the entire *Armor of God,* believers are to be constantly praying. Prayer is not regarded as part of the armor, but the believer who has on the armor is to persevere in prayer.

Romans 13:14 tells us to '...*put...on the Lord Jesus Christ*'.

This is done by prayer, for Christ is made real to us through prayer.

In order for believers to stand victoriously in the conflict – even with the complete armor – there must be constant, earnest prayer. It is through prayer of faith that the believer's armor is first put on, and then becomes effective. Since prayer is associated here with warfare, the indication is that prayer itself is part of the battle. Daniel experienced the battle of prayer. He had been praying without answer, and then he said,

> ...*behold, an hand touched me, which set me upon my knees and upon the palms of my hands. And he said unto me, O Daniel, a man greatly beloved, understand the worlds that I speak unto thee, and stand upright. For unto thee am I now sent. And when he had spoken this word unto me, I stood trembling. Then said he unto me, fear not, Daniel, or from the first day that thou didst set thine heart to understand, and to chasten thyself before thy God, the words were heard, and I am come for thy words. But the Prince of the Kingdom of Persia withstood me one and twenty days. But, lo, Michael, one of the Chief Princes, came to help me, and I remained there with the King of Persia.*

(Daniel 10:10-13)

This gives us an insight into the way principalities and powers seek to hinder answers to prayer.

Our Savior also knew of the battle of prayer for he agonized in prayer. While he was in the Garden of Gethsemane, he thought about His coming death on the cross,

> *...and being in an agony he prayed more earnestly and his sweat was as it were great drops of blood falling down to the ground.*
>
> (Luke 22:44)

The word translated "*agony*" refers to a conflict, fight or contest. Here it denotes severe emotional strain and anguish. Jesus was having an intense struggle in prayer because of the cross that loomed before him.

Prayer is a conflict in itself, and it is vital in the spiritual warfare in which every believer is involved. Notice from Ephesians 6:18 that praying and watching should be done "*with all perseverance*". This doesn't mean that we defeat Satan by working and striving in prayer, for we have already seen that Satan is a defeated foe because of Christ's work on the cross. However, our agonizing in prayer has to do with our taking our position in Christ as the victorious one. We are to "*...fight the good fight of faith*" (1 Timothy 6:12) by means of prayer.

Someone has said, "Prayer is not trying to persuade God to join us in our service for Him. It is joining Him in His service. Prayer is a true Christian laying hold, by faith, on property which Satan controls but which rightly belongs to God, and holding on until Satan lets go!"

PRAYING IN THE SPIRIT

Ephesians 6:17 tells of the "Sword of the Spirit" (vs. 18) tells of praying "In the Spirit". Just as human weapons are of no value in the spiritual warfare, (2 Corinthians 10:4), prayer that is not "*in*" the spirit is also of no value. A prayer that is lovely to listen to may not necessarily be "In the Spirit". Some believers may not know how to express themselves adequately in prayer before others, but they may be praying effectively in the spirit.

Prayer is effectual when it has its' origin with God. God sees the whole battlefield and knows the devil's plans. God decides the place and part of every soldier in the conflict. He directs the movement of the entire spiritual army. Since God sets forth definite objectives to be carried out in His eternal purpose, He must also implant in us our prayers for spiritual victory. God communicates to us through the Holy Spirit the prayers we are to pray. The Holy Spirit lays the proper burden on us and he motivates and gives us the thoughts to pray.

> *...likewise the Spirit also helpeth our infirmities, for we know not what we should pray for as we ought, but the Spirit itself maketh intercession for us with groanings which cannot be uttered.*
>
> (Romans 8:26)

So it is God who gives the deep sense of urgency for prayer and also gives assurance of victory. We do not know where Satan has placed his snares and pitfalls. But, if we are alert to the Holy Spirit, He will stimulate prayer within us so we will be forewarned and fully ready with the provided armor. We should be sensitive to the Holy Spirit's work in our lives as He prompts us to pray and gives assur-

140

ance that our prayers will be answered. Even though we do not know what to pray for, the Holy Spirit will prompt us and will pray through us. The Father, through the Spirit, motivates us to pray for what we should. (Romans 8:26-27) Then we, in the Spirit, present our petitions back to the Father in the Name of Jesus Christ. Someone has said, *"Prayer in the Spirit must be spirit-inspired, spirit-inwrought, spirit-taught, spirit-directed and spirit-energized."* Even in prayer, we can expect God to work in us to give you the desire to pray and then to energize us as we pray. (Philippians 2:13)

PRAYING CONSTANTLY

The words *"Praying Always"* (Ephesians 6:18) suggests alertness as well as praying at all times under all conditions. This is unbroken communion with the Lord, not just set times of coming to Him in prayer. It is good to have definite times set aside to spend in prayer, but throughout the day we should be talking to the Lord as we go about various tasks.

Praying constantly in the spirit has two significant implications.

It is an admission of our ignorance and impotency in spiritual conflict – we do not know what to do and we do not have the power, of ourselves, to do anything. Such prayer is heeding the words of:

> *...trust in the Lord with all thine heart, and lean not unto your own understanding. In all thy ways acknowledge Him, and He shall direct thy paths.*
> (Proverbs 3:5-6)

It reveals to the enemy that we are totally depending on God because we do not have supernatural wisdom and power. By means of prayer, we are,

...strong in the Lord, and in the power of His might.

(Ephesians 6:10)

The prayer warrior is a paradox. Toward Christ he shows conscious weakness and seeks strength and wisdom. Toward Satan he shows strength in Christ and stands firm in the place of victory.

In ourselves we can do nothing, as is evident from Christ's words,

...For without me ye can do nothing.

(John 15:5)

However, in Christ we can do all things, as Paul stated in:

...I can do all things through Christ which strengtheneth me.

(Philippians 4:13)

As we claim our position in Christ through prayers, He will always cause us to triumph. (2 Corinthians 2:14).

We are instructed to pray "*...with all prayer.*" (Ephesians 6:18)

This refers to every kind of prayer – public, private, long, short, audible, inaudible, asking, and thanking. The Bible tells us:

...stop being worried about anything, but always, in prayer and entreaty, and with thanksgiving, keep on making your wants known to God. Then,

142

through your union with Christ Jesus, the peace of God, that surpasses all human thought, will keep guard over your hearts and thoughts.

(Philippians 4:6-7)

PERSEVERING IN PRAYER

Satan fears the believer who knows how to prevail with God in prayer, for he knows that means the omnipotent power of God is being rallied against him. Because of this, Satan will use any device he can to keep us from praying. Sometimes he uses fatigue, for if we wait until the end of the day to spend time in prayer with God, we will frequently be too tired to pray. Or Satan will use lethargy and encourage us to delay talking to the Lord about our needs. Satan also uses doubt, discouragement and depression to take away our desire to pray. If these do not work, Satan may use problems at work or in the home to preoccupy our thinking and keep us from prayer. But we are to resist Satan in these attempts and are to be,

...praying always with all prayer and supplication in the spirit, and watching thereunto with all perseverance and supplication for all saints.

(Ephesians 6:18)

We are to be alert – "watching thereunto with all perseverance".

The best way the believer has of watching or keeping on the alert is through the study of the scriptures. It is from the scriptures that we learn to know God's mind, and from them we also learn how Satan may sidetrack us. We must always be on the alert and persevere in our watching.

Notice that we are to pray and watch "with all perseverance." That is, we are not to give up or become discouraged when answers to prayer are delayed. Perhaps you have been praying for something for a long time. Have you ever thought about the fact that God knows exactly when to answer that prayer? Our responsibility is to keep on praying and to trust God completely for an answer according to His will in His own time. If God has really laid something on our hearts that is His will to do; we should not pray and then wonder whether He will do it or not. We should pray and then watch how God is going to answer.

Praying for all Believers

Ephesians 6:18 tells us that we are to be praying and "watching thereunto with all perseverance and supplication for all saints'. Prayer for all the saints is necessary because we are all in the spiritual conflict together. All believers are members of the Body of Christ and the Bible says:

> *...whether one member suffer, all the members suffer with it. Or one member be honored, all the members rejoice with it.*
> (1 Corinthians 12:26)

We need to work together as a team. Remember, individuals who excel in team sports may receive much attention, but much of their success depends on their team victories. Grace is always available to those who claim it. May those of us who know charity return often to the Book of Ephesians to be reminded of our position in Him and then may we live accordingly, for this is living abundantly.

CHAPTER TWELVE

The Expected Results

If we put on "The Whole Armor of God" what results can we expect? In considering this, we should remember that the armor is available to all who know Christ and who will appropriate it by faith. No believer has an excuse for any vulnerable spot because the armor is available for full protection.

The results that can be expected when the entire armor is appropriated by faith center in the three occurrences of the word "Able" in this passage:

> ...put on the whole armor of God, that ye may be able to stand against the wiles of the devil.
> (Ephesians 6:11, 13, 16)

From this verse we see that the appropriation of the entire armor enables us to stand against the devil's craftiness. Even the weakest believer can overcome Satan by

exercising faith in Christ for each aspect of His life. God
desires that each believer have a victorious Christian life.
With Paul, we can say,

>*...thanks be unto God, which always causeth us
to triumph in Christ.*
>>(1 Corinthians 2:14)

We can also echo his words,

>*...Thanks be to God, which giveth us the victory
through our Lord Jesus Christ.*
>>(1 Corinthians 15:57)

and, we can apply Paul's conclusion:

>*...therefore, my beloved brethren, be ye steadfast,
unmovable, always abounding in the work of the
Lord, forasmuch as ye know that your labor is not
in vain in the Lord.*
>>(1 Corinthians 15:58)

So let us expect victory, not defeat. By faith we can conquer! Too many have been defeated simply because they
have gone into the spiritual conflict anticipating failure.
Let us not forget that we are "able".

The second occurrence of the word "able" is in:

>*...wherefore take unto you the whole armor of
God, that ye may be able to withstand in the evil
day, and having done all, to stand.*
>>(Ephesians 6:13)

Another result of appropriating the spiritual armor by
faith is that we will be able to stand victorious in the evil
day. The word translated "WITHSTAND" can also be
translated "RESIST", as it is in

...submit yourselves therefore to God. Resist the devil and he will flee from you.

(James 4:7)

This word is translated "RESIST" in:

...whom resist steadfast in the faith, knowing that the same afflictions are accomplished in your brethren that are in the world.

(1 Peter 5:9)

The armor enables the believer to effectively resist Satan and thus to stand victorious in the "evil day". The "evil day" probably refers to the time of severe temptations and trials.

The only way that we can successfully encounter and defeat Satan is when we are, by faith, entrenched in Christ. This is why James 4:7 first mentions that we are to submit ourselves to God before it mentions that we are to resist the devil. When we submit to Christ and depend on Him as our fortress, He will be our wall of defense.

The statement in *"...resist steadfast in the faith"* (1 Peter 5:9) reminds us that we are to stand fast in faith's victorious position. It is evident that the spiritual conflict is a fight of faith. At the end of his life, Paul charged Timothy *"...fight the good fight of faith."* (1 Timothy 6:12)

Of himself, Paul could say,

...for I am now ready to be offered, and the time of my departure is at hand. I have fought a good fight (of faith), I have finished my course, I have kept the faith. Henceforth there is laid up for me a crown of righteousness, which the Lord, a righteous judge, shall give me at that day. And not to

147

me only, but unto all them also that love His appearing.

(2 Timothy 4:6, 7)

Let us trust the Lord for every detail of our life. If we fail, let us confess our sin to Him and remember that He has promised to forgive when we confess it (1 John 1:9).

...Let us walk in the light, as He is in the light.

(1 John 1:7)

We will experience victory over Satan. As we study the Word of God we should let the light of His Word expose any sin and immediately confess it.

The third occurrence of the word "able" concerning the spiritual armor is found in:

...above all, taking the shield of faith, wherewith ye shall be able to quench all the fiery darts of the wicked one.

(Ephesians 6:16)

Thus we see another result that can be expected when we appropriate the armor by faith. We will be enabled to put out all the fire-tipped arrows of the devil. This is possible by trusting in Jesus Christ who is the shield of faith for the believer. We have carefully examined the verses previously which reveal that Christ is our shield and life and that He lives in and through us (Galatians 2:29; Colossians 23:3-4)

Christ is the shield that faith apprehends, and He stands between the believer and Satan so we need never fear. The Lord is with us at all times even as David realized (Psalm 23). As we put our trust in Him, He will protect us on every side.

148

The truth we have seen from the six pieces of armor is that each one presents different aspects of the way Jesus Christ is the protection for His own. Our responsibility is to place our confidence in Him for each step we take.

STUDY QUESTIONS

CHAPTER ONE

1. Explain the three truths in the Book of Ephesians.

2. Why can the believer expect spiritual conflict?

3. What device does Satan use to entice the believer?

4. Describe the conflict between the 'old nature' and the 'new nature'.

5. Explain why Satan is the enemy of the believer's soul.

6. What method did Herod use in his attempt to destroy Jesus?

7. How was Jesus saved from being destroyed by Herod?

8. Why does Satan attack the believers?

9. Why does Satan hate and fear Christ?

10. Explain the 'dispensational' reason for spiritual conflict.

11. What is the Holy Spirit's work in the world today?

12. Describe why the Christian does not have to live in fear.

13. What is required of a believer in order to obtain a 'position' in Christ?

14. What is the one thing a believer's position is Christ is based upon?

15. What thing can separate the Believer from Christ?

16. What is the valid promise upon which everything else is based?

CHAPTER TWO

1. Explain why 'spiritual conflict' is represented as "war"?

2. Name the five things in Paul's animated exhortation why the Christians have need for strength.

3. Why does the Christian have no strength in himself?

4. Describe how the Word (sealed book) is revealed to the believer.

5. There are two points to which the apostle Paul designs to lead us; explain each one.

6. Why is it necessary for believers to "be strong in Him"?

7. Explain why Is. 45:24 is important.

8. To what benefit to the believer is the example of David and Goliath?

9. List the 3 different classes of Christians.

10. In spiritual victories why should we be careful not to arrogate to ourselves some portion of the glory?

CHAPTER THREE

1. Who is the key figure a believer must face in conflict?

2. What part of the believer's anatomy must be changed to deal with the internal enemy?

3. What must we 'come to grips' with in order to be in a position to maintain victory?

4. For what reason did the Israelites wander in the desert for forty years?

5. Why were the Israelites ineffective for God?

6. There was one thing the new generation of Israelites did that enabled them to effectively stand against their enemies. Explain why this was important.

7. Not only was the older generation unable to go into the promised land, what else did they miss out on?

8. What two types of conflict does the victorious Christian face?

9. What binds unbelievers to Satan?

10. What is the believer's responsibility to the unbeliever?

11. Explain why there is no neutral position regarding one's relationship with Christ.

12. List the attributes for a good soldier.

13. Explain why the "attributes" are vital.

14. Through what two venues does our enemy visibly express himself?

15. Since Satan is not omnipresent, how does he wage war on believers?

16. Why are man made weapons ineffective in warfare against Satan?

17. How many 'heavens' does Paul refer to and describe each one.

18. Explain which heaven is the believer's position and why.

19. In Is. 14:12-14 name the two names that refer to Lucifer.

20. Which of the heavens does the prince of the power of the air claim domain over?

21. By what tactic does Satan use to conceal his activities?

22. Satan has two grand objectives. Explain each one and how they operate.

23. What type of devices does Satan use to lead men into sin and why?

24. How do the 'seasons' affect Satan's plan of attack?

25. How did Satan use the 'season' in his temptation of Christ?

26. Not only does Satan use 'seasons' of weariness, he also uses _____and _____.

27. Which two 'offices' will a general choose to employ to betray the enemy into his hands?

28. What lesson is learned in Mt. 16:22?

29. Of all the avenues Satan uses to lead men into sin, which is the 'most fit' instrument?

30. Explain how Satan persuaded Eve to sin against God.

31. How does he use this same cunning on all believers?

CHAPTER TEN

1. Name the piece of armor which represent the Word of God.

2. What does the 'Word' specifically refer to?

3. Describe the terms "Living Word' and "Written Word".

4. The Word is _____ _____ for the believer.

5. When Jeremiah said 'thy words were found, and I did eat them'; what was he saying?

6. God's Written Word came to us by_____.

7. God's Living Word came to us by _____.

8. The Written Word (_____) and the Living Word (_____) are inseparable.

9. The Written Word is the message of the _____ _____.

10. Why is it important to know what the scriptures say and not to just memorize them?

11. What is necessary in order to effectively use the Sword of the Spirit?

CHAPTER ELEVEN

1. In the Book of Ephesians, what reaches the highest pinnacle recorded.

2. How is the armor put on?

3. How does prayer become part of the battle?

4. How do we 'fight the good fight' of faith?

5. Read the last paragraph on page 139. How does this apply in your Christian life?

6. When is prayer effective?

7. The Father, through the Holy Spirit motivates us to pray for _____ _____ _____.

8. Prayer in the spirit must be _____ -_____, _____-_____, _____-_____, _____-_____, and _____-_____.

9. Explain the two implications of praying constantly in the spirit.

10. Explain what it means "the prayer warrior is a paradox".

CHAPTER TWELVE

1. If we put on the whole armor, what results can we expect?

2. Explain the three 'ables' in this Ephesians 6: 11, 13, 16.

3. Why should we expect victory and not defeat?

4. What stands between the believer and Satan?